THE BRUTUS REVIVAL

*Parricide and Tyrannicide
During the Renaissance*

Manfredi Piccolomini

Southern Illinois University Press
Carbondale and Edwardsville

Library of Congress Cataloging-in-Publication Data

Piccolomini, Manfredi
The Brutus revival : parricide and tyrannicide during the
renaissance / Manfredi Piccolomini
p.   cm.
Includes bibliographical references.
1. European drama—Renaissance, 1450–1600—History and criticism.
2. Assassination in literature.   3. Parricide in literature.
4. Brutus, Marcus Junius, 85?–42 B.C., in fiction, drama, poetry,
etc. I. Title.
PN1791.P5   1991
809'.93358—dc20   89-78134
ISBN 0-8093-1649-8   CIP

The paper used in this publication meets the minimum requirements of
American National Standard for Information Sciences—Permanence of
Paper for Printed Library Materials, ANSI Z39.48-1984. ∞

For my mother

Contents

Preface

ix

Acknowledgments

xiii

1. The Making of a Destiny

1

2. Brutus Carries Out His Destiny

35

3. Brutus, Destiny, and Tragedy

95

Appendix: Hamlet as a New Brutus

119

Notes

125

Bibliography

132

Index

136

Preface

The initial idea to write about Brutus came to me in the late 1970s when, as a graduate student, I heard a friend make a passing comment during a lecture about Michelangelo's double standard regarding the killer of Caesar. My friend recalled a famous dialogue by Michelangelo in which the great artist, a republican and libertarian, at once praised and condemned Brutus. He praised Brutus for having freed Rome from a potential dictator and condemned him because, subsequent to his act, a brutal civil war ensued that ended with a stronger dictatorship than that of Caesar. Michelangelo thought that if Brutus had let history take its course and Caesar accomplish his political plans, then the result would not have been historically so momentous. Once the emergency that brought Caesar to absolute power was over, the traditional republican system could have been restored.

I sympathized with Michelangelo in taking such an ambiguous position because he so dramatically expressed the opposition between the ideal point of view—killing Caesar no matter what the consequence—and the pragmatic one—allowing Caesar to fulfill his program. Also, although I was living in the United States, my mind was often occupied by events in Italy, the country that I had left a few years earlier and to which I returned very often. In those days Italy was plagued by the scourge of terrorism that culminated in the killing of Moro, the country's leading political figure.

The killing of Moro had many metaphorical similarities with the killing of Caesar. In both cases an Oedipal impulse had been clearly at work. Moro too had become a sort of "father of the country," the man who had mastered Italy's reconstruction and new prosperity after the disaster of World War II. But his personal power had become so overwhelming that it inhibited any opportunity for change and growth in the political system. For all practical purposes Moro ran the country almost as his own kingdom. In the terrorists' minds the killing of the "father" would have set change in motion. Instead, as in Sophocles' drama, it brought about a tragedy. The masses, reacting to the killing of Moro as two thousand years earlier the Roman people had reacted to the killing of Caesar, did not accept a murderous act as a chance for positive political rejuvenation. When the terrorists, like Brutus, tried to force upon the people the acknowledgment that with the death of the dictator a new political era was possible, the killers of the tyrant became the victims of the general will.

As an undergraduate student at the University of Florence, I had witnessed the intellectual origins of Italian terrorism. Leftist students called for a rebellion against all powers that maintained the status quo. It was time to leave the classroom and the library and to embrace the liberating potential of the machine gun. Certain historical situations arise, they claimed, when the duty of the intellectual is to take action. The bloodbath, not the force of reason, would change the world. Like Don Quixote, the Italian terrorists had read and misunderstood too many books. The myth of violent revolution, of brute force eliminating in one act the stalemates of shrewd politicking, became the terrorists' guiding principle.

I was drawn to study the origins, both cultural and historical, of the intricate political situation developing before my eyes. I thought that the best way of understanding these complex problems was to go back to Brutus to see if the killer of Caesar could function as an archetype for all rebels and plotters. As his was the most famous tyrannicide of history, the one about whom the most histories, biographies, commentaries, stories, novels, plays, and poems have been written, I thought that in the Brutus figure and in the Brutus legend I could find most of the elements—cultural, psychological, and political—that color any attempt conducted by one or more conspirators to subvert power by surprise and violent action.

That books, even those on historical and literary subjects, are ultimately the product of a direct life experience could not be more true than in this case. Wanting to study the cultural origins of political terrorism, in Brutus I discovered a powerful example, a mythologized historical figure whose name and actions were often recalled whenever political circumstances presented predicaments similar to his own.

In Brutus I also detected the intellectual turned man of action, who allows historical and literary examples to guide his political life almost entirely. Before becoming a mythical symbol of the just citizen rebelling against the unjust tyrant, the learned Brutus also tried to find in past Roman history and in philosophical wisdom guidance for his new role as a political activist.

Therefore, while covering theories of parricide and tyrannicide from Dante to the High Renaissance and examining how Italian conspiracies formed the basis for the rich theatrical production on the Brutus theme in French, Italian, and English drama, my book has a special focus. I should like to emphasize how the Brutus myth became an inspiration and a guide for all the self-proclaimed just citizens rebelling against unjust tyrants. My ultimate goal is to show what an important role ideas and patterns of action derived from history and literature play in the course of human events or, to say it more simply, how often life imitates art.

Acknowledgments

To Professor Eric Havelock, who recently passed away, I owe the fundamental principles of this book. Through my translation into Italian of one of his works and the long conversations with him that ensued, I learned that human events are always the consequence of a cluster of historical, cultural, literary, and psychological themes that become part of the collective subconscious of a culture. He convinced me that the happenings of history are secretly guided by subconscious myths. If this work achieves any of its purported goals, then it is because the unusual meeting of the eminent scholar of Greek literature with the young aspiring student of the Renaissance led to unexpected results. Because of Havelock's inspiring guidance, the comparative and thematic approach of my study embraces history, literature, political science, and to a lesser extent, the fine arts and leads to a view of culture and human events interlocked in a circularity where cause and effect are practically interchangeable. My greatest regret in publishing this work is that he is no longer here to see it, as I would like him to realize that the scholar can exert an influence well beyond the confines of his or her official field.

To Hans Baron, who upon receiving a paper always started reading from the footnotes, I owe the generous and severe criticism of my first, very confused writings on the Renaissance.

To Professor Daniel Javitch, who gave me sound practical advice on how to structure my manuscript, I am indebted for the important lesson that form is also substance.

To Lisa Bayer and Keith Hollaman, who tried, if ever possible, to make my Italianate English somewhat readable, go my sincere thanks.

For their unperturbed and nonchalant assistance I also thank the librarians of the overstaffed upstairs reading room at the Biblioteca Nazionale in Florence where I did most of my research.

My mother, to whom the book is dedicated, deserves a special place among my acknowledgments for having provided the support and the encouragement without which life, in the early years of my academic career, would have been a lot less amenable.

And finally I thank my impatient wife, who never knew what was in store for her when she married me and learned the hard way about the inevitable neurosis associated with the writing process. I am sure that by now she is resigned to the fact that there is more to come.

THE BRUTUS REVIVAL

1

The Making of a Destiny

Dante Rediscovers Brutus

If Marcus Brutus can claim to be one of the historical figures of Roman classicism who received the greatest attention during the Renaissance, he owes it mainly to Dante. Dante put him once again into the arena of moral and political debate and transmitted his historical persona to the Humanists of the Renaissance. They, in turn, constantly referred to Brutus in their writings and tracts in order to discuss, first, the basic themes of moral philosophy and, second, political theories and practice. Finally, the late Renaissance civilization developed a sense of tragedy primarily through Brutus that, I shall try to demonstrate, culminated in Shakespeare's *Julius Caesar* and *Hamlet*.

The process of transmission and evolution of the Brutus figure was, however, not a simple one. The writers of the Italian Renaissance mainly composed scholarly works and were less inclined to focus on freer, more literary creations. Renaissance scholars interpreted other texts—those coming from the Greco-Roman tradition—and therefore what the Humanists wrote about Brutus depended in part on which classical texts, in those pre-Gutenberg days, were available at that particular time. During the Renaissance classical authors were brought back to light only little by little throughout the fourteenth, fifteenth, and sixteenth centuries. Among those writers whose work became available after centuries of oblivion, many, including Cicero, Virgil, Seneca, Lucan, Plutarch, Suetonius, Marcus Aurelius, and Appian, discussed the actions of Brutus and considered Caesar's fight for absolute power and his final doom, along with the civil war that followed, the central and most crucial points of Roman history. There

1

were differing views among them, depending on their own political inclinations and allegiances, but few classicists denied that the Ides of March had a significant impact on the events that followed. When analyzing Humanist writings on this subject, prime consideration must be given therefore to the individual classical sources that were, on every occasion, the objects of the discussion.

Whoever wrote about Brutus during the Renaissance and discussed his controversial role in the political struggle that changed the course of Roman history was motivated by more than the need to ponder the moral and political conditions of that ancient time. The rediscovery of classical themes and history was also a learning experience for the Humanists that involved the desire to revive ancient forms of civility and morality that they considered to be superior to their own. Classical authors were, after a medieval pun often used by Dante, not only authors but also the symbols of authority.[1]

However, the classics did not constitute the only source for the discussions on Brutus during the Renaissance. Dante was a gigantic figure standing between the ancients and the moderns, and his assessment of Brutus was too powerful and too unambiguous to be ignored. Ironically, the fact that Dante was not familiar with many classical writers dealing with the Brutus character was considered of little or no importance. The Humanists did not even take this fact into consideration because *The Divine Comedy* was such a monumental work. It would have been a paradox to dismiss one of the poem's most poignant statements simply because the statement lacked historical documentation. As often happens, assertions from a source of authority need not be documented to be taken seriously!

Dante's condemnation of Brutus is unambiguous, although on initial inspection, it may seem quite contradictory. Brutus is depicted in the last canto of the *Inferno* as he is being chewed in one of Lucifer's three mouths, along with his companion-in-arms, Cassius, and Judas. The lowest place in hell, where Dante starts his ascent to purgatory, appears to be worthy only of Caesar's killers and of Judas, who in the late medieval tradition was believed to be the betrayer of Christ and the cause of his death. The only difference between the punishments of Brutus and Cassius and that of Judas consists of the way in which the three are subjected to Lucifer's devouring jaws. While Judas has his head buried deep inside the devil's mouth, the upper part of the bodies of Brutus and Cassius hang out, so they enjoy the questionable privilege of contemplating the frozen darkness of the pit of hell:

Each mouth devoured a sinner clenched within,
Frayed by the fangs like flax beneath a brake;
Three at a time he tortured them for sin.

But all the bites the one in front might take
Were nothing to the claws that flayed his hide
And sometimes stripped his back to the last flake.

"That wretch up there whom keenest pangs divide
Is Judas called Iscariot," said my lord,
"His head within, his jerking legs outside;

As for the pair whose heads hang hitherward:
From the black mouth the limbs of Brutus sprawl—
See how he writhes and utters never a word;

And strong-thewed Cassius is his fellow-thrall.
But come; for night is rising on the world
Once more; we must depart; we have seen all."[2]

To Dante, Judas, Cassius, and Brutus are the worst sinners. In
the case of Brutus, the sins of assassination and betrayal of which he
was guilty are not only sins committed against another human being
but also are sins involving a more universal and cosmological realm,
directed as they were against Julius Caesar. To turn against Caesar—
Caesar representing in Dante's view the earthly counterpart of God,
the one who guides humankind's earthly existence—is to rebel against
God's will, to upset his historical design. Dante also expressed his
ideas about Caesar and about the imperial rule that Caesar was preparing in his political treatise *De Monarchia* (*On Monarchy*), where the
concept of the Empire as a supreme form of government is justified by
a number of classical authorities.[3] Among these sources was Dante's
favorite author and his guide to salvation, Virgil, whose *Fourth Eclogue* was interpreted during the Middle Ages as the prophecy of the
coming of a new political and religious order centered around the
Empire and the Christian faith. As Dante writes:

The world is inclined towards a state of perfection only when
supreme justice reigns in it. Therefore Virgil, willing to celebrate his century, sung in his *Eclogues*:

Iam redit et Virgo, redeunt Saturnia regna.

"Virgin" was in fact the name of Justice, also called "Astrea";
the "kingdom of Saturn" were those happy times also known as
the "Golden Age." Justice is supreme only under the Monarch:
therefore the existence of Monarchy or Empire is necessary to
the perfect disposition of the world.[4]

This highly symbolic interpretation of a line in Virgil's famous
Fourth Eclogue that fuses virginity—the virginity dear to the Christians—and justice, the age of Saturn and the Golden Age, should leave
no doubts as to Dante's moral framework in his condemnation of
Brutus. Brutus, responsible for betraying Caesar, who had been so
generous with him, also took it upon himself to wage war against an
idea of worldly order above human control. The Empire is the one
political institution totally beyond human responsibility. If citizens
are indeed responsible for the proper ordering of the civil body in
which they live, if they are indeed also political beings, their activities
in this sphere must be limited to their city or their country. The
Empire is a much wider, much more universal concept. The Empire
is the earthly counterpart of the city of God. That God chose the
imperial period for Christ's birth is an additional piece of symbolic
evidence that the establishment of one ruler was willed by a superior
power. Turning against Caesar, who primarily initiated the political
events that led to the establishment of imperial rule, was therefore
considered an act against destiny. And destiny, in the Christian view,
is not guided by chance as it was for the Greek and Latin atomists.
It is not even mysterious as it was for the Stoics. It is revealed and
guided by God. The medieval Christian view of the world does not
allow any room for hubris and therefore for tragedy, the natural
consequence of hubris for the Greeks. Christian theologians and
philosophers, Dante among them, believed that their worldview represented a step forward, a measurable progress, from Greek and
Roman culture. The concept of tragedy was at the center of this
progress.

The psychological, political, and philosophical motivations that
compel the individual to adopt the role of the savior are of no interest
to the medieval mind. It is not up to the individual to take sides in
the struggle between virtue and sin, order and chaos, good and evil,
when the struggle involves the ultimate values of existence and is
destined to reveal a higher truth. God is supreme virtue, supreme
order, and supreme good. For Dante the process leading to the
establishment of the Empire was a step forward on the road to

perfection, another major advance towards the kingdom of God. Brutus' murder of Caesar was an attempt to stop the process and the fulfillment of God's will and was therefore doomed to failure from the start.

Ulysses and Horace as Reverse Role Models

From a philosophical point of view, Dante's Brutus bears comparison to Dante's Ulysses. Dante transforms Ulysses, another great hero of the classical world whose exploits, narrated by Homer, inspired major works of classical literature, so that his historical and literary significance may be judged in accordance with Christian morality. Dante changes the traditional story in his version and makes Ulysses guilty of hubris for attempting to challenge the very limits that God had imposed on the world. In Homer's *Odyssey*, as well as in the following classical tradition, Ulysses is represented as a crafty, intelligent, and shrewd hero who uses his talents to return home after the end of the Trojan War. He does not tempt destiny; he only cunningly overcomes the obstacles that destiny places between him and his goal to return to his home and family on the island of Ithaca. From a more symbolic point of view, the classical Ulysses appears to be a centripetal hero, one who treasures his origins and his homeland and wants to return to them. He is not compelled by the need to search for new adventures and certainly does not want to discover a new world. He simply strives to regain his old world that he was temporarily forced to abandon when he joined the Greek forces during the Trojan War. With Dante Ulysses becomes a centrifugal figure, strongly characterized by the pioneering and entrepreneurial attitudes that we have come to consider typical of our own modern times. Attracted by the unknown, he wants to violate the boundaries of what should be known. Dante places Ulysses in the twenty-sixth canto of the *Inferno* and establishes the grounds for Ulysses' punishment with a story that the poet creates. Dante has Ulysses confess that instead of returning home to his family with a small group of followers he sailed beyond the Columns of Hercules (today's Strait of Gibraltar), which until Columbus' time were considered God's imposed limits to the known world. Because of his daring attempt, because of his hubris, Ulysses and his group encounter death on the high seas while sailing east towards an unknown land that they imagined was a new earthly paradise.

Dante may have modeled his transformation of the classical legend of Ulysses on stories about medieval explorers who dared venture beyond the Mediterranean Sea and never returned. He may have found Ulysses' determination to overcome any difficulty suitable for his message, but the message is nevertheless very clear: people are not to violate the limits imposed by God.

Horace, the poet of the middle way, who preached containment and viewed the happy life as based on self-knowledge and the small pleasures of daily existence, may well have been, long before the Church Fathers, the model for Dante's condemnation of Ulysses. In the second poem of the first book of his *Epistole (Epistles)* Horace tries to convince a friend, Maximus Lollius, that a simple life based on just what is necessary to guarantee a sufficient maintenance is the real, virtuous life. Horace maintains that the opposite of this ideal is represented by Ulysses as an "example and symbol of what virtue and wisdom could be, Ulysses, after winning at Troy, wanted to know the cities and the ways of many other peoples, and suffered all kinds of travails on the vast seas, trying to return home with his companions."[5]

In order to show how Horace's description of Ulysses, along with Seneca's, about whom we will speak later, constitutes the basis for Dante's version, one must consider the larger context of the poem—only then will the negative connotations emerge. Horace is indeed proposing a moderate model of life, one of simplicity and of containment. At the same time, while realizing that Ulysses can in no way fit this ideal, Horace uses him as an example of classical virtue and wisdom. This is only an apparent contradiction: through certain works such as this of Horace, along with the writings of the Stoic philosophers of the late Republic and early Empire, virtue and wisdom acquire a moral, rather than a material, connotation. The change in these terms' meanings from classical and tragic to modern and ethical possibly occurred during Horace's lifetime and their employment in his description of Ulysses may constitute also an indictment of the more archaic meaning. Horace was in fact a member of the anti-Caesarean party and a follower of Brutus. Along with Brutus he initially wanted to oppose Caesar's revolution with the power of arms.

Brutus' armed struggle to stop the destruction of the Roman republican liberties and to prevent the concentration of power into the hands of one man was a classical struggle aimed at restoring the past through force and at bringing back a political condition—the Republic—that was quickly degenerating. Brutus' ability to do so was his strength, his virtue. If Brutus failed and died like a Roman should, Horace, who is believed to have deserted the battlefield and to have placed his life above his ideals, did not. Following that dubious act Horace accepted the new political realities like many other former republicans. His priorities became less political and more moral, leading him to believe that virtue is realized through the cultivation of one's soul. If the destiny of Brutus is classical to the end, tragic in all its details, Horace's is not, a fact that may well explain Dante's sympathy for the latter rather than for the former.

In Horace's poems many elements, based on and derived from Stoicism, are definitely pre-Christian. First Horace displays a contempt for the world and all worldly matters that seems to anticipate a medieval monastic ideal. Moreover, his poems contain the message that history and external events should not constitute an impediment to individual human development, which can only be attained through self-knowledge. Most of all, Horace feels that individual will and power—one's virtue—cannot modify the course of history.

Everyone Is Guilty: Stoic Theories of Death and Suicide

Whether guided by God or not, Stoic destiny was at least a very mysterious force, one that could not be opposed or controlled by the simple exercise of virtue as power. On the contrary, the Stoics believed that virtue considered as a quality of the soul—a power belonging to the interior rather than to the exterior—could help humankind live happily despite contrary external events.

In the case of Ulysses, Dante adopts a legend untrue to its Homeric prototype. In the case of Brutus, the poet takes history at face value and places him in hell for killing Caesar. However, Dante's treatment of Brutus is layered with many literary references, making it one of the most difficult and complex episodes of *The Divine Comedy* to interpret. In order to properly understand Dante's Brutus one must first understand the poet's primary literary sources for the episode, his use of them, and the complex relationship that Dante indirectly establishes between Brutus and his step-uncle, the Stoic philosopher Cato.

Despite the fact that Cato was a pagan who committed suicide— a serious sin in Dante's Christian moral system—he appears in *The Divine Comedy* in the first canto of *Purgatory* as the first symbol of salvation that the reader encounters. Lucan's epic *Pharsalia* is gener-

ally accepted as Dante's main source for the Brutus and Cato characters. Also a republican, Lucan, who lived in the first century A.D.,
participated in the famous conspiracy against the emperor Nero. And
just like Brutus after his political design had failed, Lucan committed
suicide when his participation in the plot against the emperor was
uncovered. His poem, dealing with the civil war against Caesar, is
full of premonitions of the author's own destiny. As in a tragedy
whose plot is predetermined by a cruel destiny, the main theme of
the *Pharsalia* is death and the way in which the different characters
in the play encounter it. Lucan himself, cut off by his own suicide,
was unable to complete the epic.

The events in the *Pharsalia* move at a slow pace, with ideas rather
than facts at the center of the work. They are the basic ideas of Stoic
philosophical meditation: virtue, destiny, and duty in the face of
uncontrollable events. Dante's keen interest in the *Pharsalia* must
have been motivated by the special role that Cato plays in the epic.
In the *Il Convivio* Dante calls Cato the "glorious Cato"[6] and in *The
Divine Comedy* places him, despite his suicide, at the opening of the
Purgatory as a guide to moral and spiritual salvation.

As he comments on the events of the civil war, sometimes speaking
with his own poetic voice and sometimes with the voice of Cato,
Lucan revolutionizes all traditional concepts of Roman morality and
turns what was a struggle for political power into a battle between
opposing moral principles and ideas. Therefore the grueling strife
that characterized the end of the Roman Republic and the birth of
the Empire becomes in the *Pharsalia* an ethical contest. If indeed
Cato's Stoic teachings dealt mainly with a higher understanding of
the concept of virtue and with the need to overcome the fear of death,
the central point of the *Pharsalia* is the contrast between virtue as
passive detachment and virtue as active involvement in the course of
contingent historical events. Obviously virtue as passivity entails the
belief that life is temporary and transitory, just a passing experience
during which people must prepare for eternity: "Death is but a point
in the midst of continuous life."[7] Caesar's struggle for absolute power
relied on the traditional Roman belief—also a Homeric belief—that
strength is virtue. To him the strongest was the most virtuous in the
struggle.

In the *Pharsalia* Lucan dwells at length on Brutus' vacillations
about what should be his role in the civil war. Should he side with
Caesar or with Pompeius? Which side is closer to the Stoic ideal of
virtue that he learned to respect from the teachings of his step-uncle

Cato? In an address to Cato, Brutus clearly spells out the moral dichotomies that are clouding Rome's destiny:

> Virtue, long ago driven out and banished from every land, finds in you her remaining support, and will never be dislodged from your breast by any turn of fortune; do you therefore guide my hesitation and fortify my weakness with your unerring strength. Let others follow Pompeius Magnus or Caesar's arms—Brutus will own no leaders but Cato. Are you the champion of peace, keeping your path unshaken amid a tottering world? Or have you resolved to stand with the arch-criminals and take your share in the disaster of a mad world, and so clear the civil war of guilt? Each man is carried away to wicked warfare by motives of his own—some by crimes of private life and fear of the laws if peace be kept; others by the need to drive away hunger by the sword and to bury bankruptcy under the destruction of the world. None has been driven to arms by mere impulse: they have been bought by a great bribe to follow the camp; do you alone choose war for its own sake? What good was it to stand firm so many years, untouched by the vices of a profligate age? This will be your sole reward for the virtue of a lifetime—that war that finds others already guilty, will make you guilty at last. Heaven forbid that this fatal strife should have power to stir your hands also to action. Javelins launched by your arm will not hurtle through the indistinguishable cloud of missiles; and, in order that all that virtue may not spend itself in vain, all the hazard of war will hurl itself in vain upon you; for who, though staggering beneath another's stroke, will not wish to fall by your sword and make you guilty? Fitter than war for you is peaceful life and tranquil solitude; so the stars of heaven roll on for ever unshaken in their courses. The part of air nearest earth is fired by thunderbolts, and the low-lying places of the world are visited by gales and long flashes of flame; but Olympus rises above the clouds. It is heaven's law, that small things are troubled and distracted, while great things enjoy peace. What joyful news to Caesar's ear, that so great a citizen has joined the fray! He will never resent your preference of his rival, of Pompey's camp to his own; for, if Cato countenances civil war, he countenances Caesar also more than enough. When half the Senate, when the consuls and other nobles, mean to wage war under a leader who holds no office, the temptation is

strong; but, if Cato too submit like these to Pompey, Caesar will be the only free man left on earth. If however, we resolve to bear arms in defence of our country's laws and to maintain freedom, you behold in me one who is not now the foe of Caesar or Pompey, though I shall be the foe of the conqueror when war is over.[8]

Brutus' hesitations between the guilty parties, the Caesareans and the Pompeians, attain in this speech a meaning that clearly transcends the contingent matter under discussion. More than a strife between two opposing parties, the civil war is for Lucan symptomatic of a sick political situation that is afflicting the city of Rome. In other words, the civil war is the external manifestation of collective sin: "Each man is carried away to wicked warfare by motives of his own— some by crimes of private life and fear of the laws if peace be kept."

The underlying theme is that of Greek tragedy. The pollution and the sickness—*polluta domus* (a home polluted) are the exact words used in Latin by Lucan—that pervade the entire civil body are inevitably going to cause the doom and destruction of all parties involved. Within this tragic setting, innocence and virtue can play no role, and the virtuous person cannot change the course of events— "What good was it to stand firm so many years, untouched by the vices of a profligate age?" In his long and dramatic speech Brutus is not asking himself and Cato whether he should side with Caesar or Pompey, but he is questioning the very meaning of participation and involvement in a situation whose outcome is already predetermined. Virtue has no role to play in the scenario. The winner, whoever he is, will be an evil one. Brutus' doubts call into question a philosophical rather than a practical matter: What is the meaning of action when its result will be evil? However, Lucan seems to want Brutus' implication that even Cato's detachment from the "vices of a profligate age" cannot improve the situation to serve as a metaphor for the human condition as seen through the eyes of a Stoic.

The city is diseased down to its very foundation and to take part in its political struggle is to take part in collective guilt. Just as in Greek tragedy in which innocent sinners inherit the guilt of their fathers, to be a Roman at the crucial time of the civil war is, from a Stoic point of view, equal to being a sinner. But Brutus wants to act; he sees action as the only possibility although he does not know how to act. In Lucan's moral agony Brutus' vision is such that he is unable to see any alternatives to siding either with Caesar or Pompey, and this is why Cato, in another long speech, compels Brutus to make up his mind. Brutus' final decision to side with Pompey rather than with Caesar, despite the fact that Pompey had killed Brutus' father and Caesar was his mother's lover, is the consequence of this highly philosophical speech by Cato:

> Brutus, I allow that civil war is the worst wickedness; but virtue will follow fearless wherever destiny summons her. It will be a reproach to the gods, that they have made even me guilty. Who would choose to watch the starry vault falling down and to feel no fear himself? or to sit with folded hands, when high heaven was crashing down and the earth shaking with the confused weight of a collapsing firmament? If nations unknown, if kings who reign in another clime beyond the seas, join the madness of Italy and the standards of Rome, shall I alone dwell in peace? Heaven keep far from me this madness, that the fall of Rome, which will stir by her disaster the Dahae and the Getae, should leave me indifferent! When a father is robbed of his sons by death, grief itself bids him lead the long funeral train to the grave; he is fain to thrust his hands into the doleful fires, and himself to hold the smoky torch where the lofty pyre rises. So never shall I be torn away before I embrace the lifeless body of my country; and I will follow to the grave the mere name and empty ghosts of Freedom. So be it! Let Rome pay atonement in full to the pitiless gods, and let no man's life be denied to the claim of war! But would it were possible for me, condemned by the powers of heaven and hell, to be the scapegoat for the nation! As hordes of foemen bore down Decius when he had offered his life, so may both armies pierce this body, may the savages from the Rhine aim their weapons at me; may I be transfixed by every spear, and may I stand between and inter-cept every blow dealt in this war! Let my blood redeem the nations, and my death pay the whole penalty incurred by the corruption of Rome. If the nations are willing to bear the yoke and resent not harsh tyranny, why should they die? Aim your swords at me alone, at me who fights a losing battle for despised law and justice. My blood, mine only, will bring peace to the people of Italy and end their sufferings; the would-be tyrant need wage no war, once I am gone. Why should I not follow the standard of the nation and Pompey as my leader? And yet I know full well that, if fortune favor him, he too looks forward

to mastery over the world. Let me then serve in his victorious army, and prevent him from thinking that he has conquered for himself alone.[9]

How does Lucan's treatment of Brutus and Cato relate to Dante? Dante's reading of and interest in the *Pharsalia* probably had little or nothing to do with the more tragic and dramatic aspects of the poem. Dante's severe condemnation of Brutus is a clear indication that the Christian poet did not subscribe to a view of Brutus as a hero torn by moral dilemmas. Dante's fascination with Lucan's epic is due to the prophetic vision constantly present in the poem. Lucan's is an omniscient poetic point of view that allows the author to predict things to come despite another narrative level in which the outcome is constantly put in jeopardy by the unfolding of the tragic plot. This supernatural and divine omniscience corresponds quite well with Dante's Christian view of history and of historical development. While on one side Lucan described the civil war as a struggle in which different moralities and ambitions radically opposed one faction against the other as in a tragedy, on the other he presented the entire struggle as having a predetermined outcome. This method is not as much a matter of contradiction as it is of two different narrative styles being employed at the same time. On one level the tragic mode portrays and describes a struggle between two opposing groups with an uncertain outcome. On the other, the Stoic, pre-Christian, omniscient mode places its priorities on the ethical value of the outcome and, as such, is totally indifferent to a judgment concerning the contrasting parties. What counts, from this latter point of view, is that the final outcome of the fight will be the victory of evil.

In a particularly dramatic battle scene that takes place in the seventh book of the poem, Lucan captures Brutus as he is approaching Caesar to kill him. The poet feels that it is appropriate to intervene in the action as the voice of destiny and to intercept Brutus, at least for the present. Claiming that fate has not yet played out all its cards and that Caesar has not yet reached the pinnacle of his fortune, Lucan calls on Brutus to postpone his act:

> O glory of Rome, last hope of the Senate and last scion of a house famous throughout history, rush not too rashly through the midst of the enemy, nor seek to anticipate the doom of Philippi: death will come to you in a Pharsalia of your own. Your design against Caesar's life is bootless here: not yet has

he attained the tyrant's stronghold; not yet has he risen beyond the lawful summit of human greatness that dwarfs all other things; and therefore he has not earned from destiny so glorious a death.[10]

These lines show quite clearly that the *Pharsalia* functions on one level as a tragic story with a plot, while the second level portrays the course of events as seen by God's omniscient eye. On one side an open-ended story tainted by tragedy is told, its outcome still unknown. On the other side events are narrated *sub specie aeternitatis* (from the point of view of eternity) as if having an inevitable outcome. While on the first level Brutus is seen as a free individual striving to succeed in his mission against Caesar, on the other he appears as destiny's puppet on his way to political failure and moral damnation. This second aspect of the *Pharsalia* attracted Dante and influenced his handling of the Brutus figure in *The Divine Comedy*.

Lucan's personal poetic intervention in the plot in the passage quoted above, to stop his character Brutus from killing Caesar before the proper time, should be read as the poet's indication that Brutus is not free to act according to his will, just like all other characters in the story. In a tragedy with no way out, all participants in the struggle must stay the course; the cards must be played out as destiny has established. The only exit, from a moral if not political point of view, is Cato's, who chooses to let history take its course and anticipates the freedom, maybe in the new life to come, that will come after death by suicide.

In the *Pharsalia* Lucan places an unprepared Brutus in a tragic situation and lets him run to his doom in a state of absolute blindness. Cato's role is quite different. In his answer to Brutus' questions that have already been outlined, the Stoic philosopher describes his role in terms that anticipate the Christian practice of martyrdom: "Let my blood redeem the nations, and my death pay the whole penalty incurred by the corruption of Rome."

When Dante decided to take up in his own poem the characters of Cato and Brutus, with the glorification of the former as a symbol of martyrdom and the condemnation of the latter, he was basically repeating some fundamental cultural stereotypes of the first and the second century A.D. Interestingly, there is no evidence of Dante being familiar with Plutarch's biography of Cato, the work that more than any other turns Cato's death into a legend of martyrdom, with many similarities to that of Socrates.

The three centuries between 100 B.C. and A.D. 200 witnessed the great moment of Roman philosophy. As political life became virtually controlled by one ruler, the old republican and aristocratic class found in philosophy both a consolation and an escape from tyranny. Brutus may well have continued to pursue his dream by trying to find a role for the virtuous individual under the yoke of tyranny. Cato found in self-knowledge and then in death the solution against the evils of one ruler's abolition of freedom. In the second chapter of *De constantia sapientis* by the great Stoic philosopher Seneca, a work almost certainly known by Dante, Cato is presented as the absolute example of the virtuous inidividual because he does not allow external events and adverse fortune to affect him:

> No man of wisdom can suffer evil or offense. The immortal Gods have moreover given us in Cato the clearest example of the man of wisdom, more than Ulysses and Hercules in the preceding centuries. Our Stoics, in fact, said that those who have wisdom are those who are not defeated by labors, who despise pleasure and repel fear. Cato did not struggle with beasts, which is the duty of the hunter or the farmer, nor did he chase monsters with fire and sword, nor did he live in times where the world was believed to rest on one man's shoulders. With ancient credulity having been defeated and living in times of greater critical intelligence, Cato fought against ambition and evils under many guises, and against the lust for power that the entire world divided among three men could not have satiated. He stood alone against the vices of the country that was degenerating and falling under its own weight. As much as he could he tried to prevent the fall of the Republic, until he himself was drawn into the ruin that he had fended off for such a long time, and immediately two things that could not be divided died together: Cato did not survive liberty, nor did liberty survive Cato.[11]

Seneca inserts the praise of Cato's virtues in a passage in which he evaluates the meaning of Greek classical culture. In that passage Seneca—the "modern" philosophical author of letters and of consolations directed to his friends who taught that in order to live a happy and virtuous life one must first of all conquer the fear of death—compares Cato to Ulysses and Hercules. Two "old-fashioned" heroes, famous for exploits made possible by their physical strength, are here set face-to-face with Cato. The difference between the world of Cato and that of Hercules and of Ulysses is explained by the opposition of critical intelligence to ancient credulity. The modern virtuous individual differs from the classical hero because of a new consciousness. Mythological and Homeric characters act and react according to preestablished patterns of behavior and rules transmitted to them by an ancient tradition and are not able to reflect critically upon their actions. The modern thinker is able to consciously make a decision when confronted with situations that could just as easily have been confronted according to the traditional, automatic pattern of behavior. The conscious individual is capable of breaking the cycle of repetition, of not necessarily being motivated by the example of the endless catalog of similar reactions to similar situations encountered in archaic cultures.

The principal aspect of what in anthropology has come to be known as the archaic classical mentality, sometimes called the primitive mentality, is domination by the collective unconscious and deprivation of individuality and awareness of one's own self. In this situation the individual consciousness is submerged by collective rules of behavior established through tradition and constantly reconfirmed by the social environment. This mentality functions only through repetition. It is incapable of creating any sort of inner progress or sense of self-improvement and reacts to external stimuli according to old models. In archaic societies patterns of behavior are coordinated by the many gods who symbolize the rules of action and who function as models of behavior. These gods have nothing in common with the god foreshadowed by Cato and Seneca, the god revealed to Dante and depicted in his writing. In more modern terms, derived from moral philosophy rather than from theology, one could say that the archaic mentality lacks the sense of free will.

Dante's condemnation of Brutus and admiration of Cato as a symbol of salvation are based mainly on this point. According to Dante, Brutus chose to wage war against Caesar because Caesar was subverting a political order that drew its moral justification and legitimacy from the past. Brutus felt responsible for reviving the old republican order because his frame of mind prevented him from seeing anything positive coming from the Republic's decay. The solution to the troubles of his times, Brutus believed, was in the restoration of the past order.

Archaic classical culture reduces behavior and its models to schemes and symbols that can be orally transmitted and easily recognized in order to be adopted as models for action. The creation of new models and possibilities through the exercise of experimentation and individual freedom is not encouraged. The archaic classical person is born into a scenario whose rules have already been set by tradition and in which he or she is requested to play a part according to the script. Improvisation, to continue with the theatrical metaphor, is not promoted and will not be promoted until about the time of Seneca. Like Platonism in Greece, Stoicism in Rome was a revolution against traditional values.

While the Stoics spoke of freedom and virtue in philosophical terms, they also spoke of the soul and Plato's theories about its immortality. In Lucretius' *De rerum natura*, an Epicurean work reflecting many Stoic principles, the author claims that only the *animum* (mind) is capable of overcoming the fear of death.[12] It would be an exaggeration to believe that this *animum*, at times defined as a vital wind, is equal to the soul of the Christians that, after its release from the body, awaits a final judgment. But Lucretius and the Stoics do represent a step in the Christian direction. For them, as for the Christians, the virtuous life is a process of learning that leads to a higher level of truth. It is only a mental process, one that requires a lifetime of dedication to knowledge. Just as for the ancients great acts of heroism were rewarded with immortality in the Elysian Fields, the virtuous life of the Stoics could anticipate a higher level of understanding somehow continued after death. The Stoics discussed immortality at length, yet never decided about the immortality of the soul or the way in which immortality manifests itself. The main theme of Stoicism—that human experience is extremely limited and its limitations must be overcome through an understanding of higher truths—carried with it the conviction that the mind and the soul could better reach such an understanding when they have been physically freed from the body, their mortal frame. Despite the lack of a systematic doctrine, common to most ancient philosophical traditions, there is no doubt that the Stoics viewed death as a liberation. If *virtus* (virtue) and *sapientia* (knowledge) were a step towards *libertas* (freedom), then *mors* (death) was the point when the entire mystery of existence would unfold itself, when knowledge and freedom would finally reveal themselves.

In reference to the Brutus-Cato problem and the way it is treated by Dante, it is also interesting to note that the Stoics believed that a higher level of understanding and a different view of happiness were achieved through a total reformation of the self. This belief is in fact the greatest legacy of Stoicism to the modern world. For the Stoics the model of perfection is no longer placed in the past, whether this past is the Golden Age or the happy times of political freedom the Romans enjoyed under the old republican rulers. In fact the very idea of perfection as a condition derived from past models is no longer that important in late Roman philosophy, which replaced it with a faith in the possibilities of experiment and change. Stoic philosophy does not promise a reward if the good path is followed, as did traditional religious beliefs. The individual is not asked to follow the traditional models of behavior, but to experiment with new ways, in the hope that they would bring about a new condition and a higher level of existence, both during life and after death.

This belief had great influence on the social and political transformations that took place in Rome around the time of the civil war. Caesar's dictatorship was not seen as a form of tyranny but as a political order with a higher moral standing. Clearly this idea is what Caesar's dictatorship represented for Dante, who thought that the Empire was the earthly counterpart of the Kingdom of God. However, it did not represent the same thing for Cato, who chose an alternative to Caesar's abolition of freedom by committing suicide. Brutus, from a Stoic point of view, got everything wrong. He fought Caesar in order to restore the old system and to bring back a political order that he believed to be far superior simply because it was the system of the past and of tradition. Seneca condemns Brutus in strictly Stoic terms, the same ones used by Dante, in a chapter of *De beneficiis* where he discusses Caesar's pardon of Brutus at the end of the civil war:

> This is the usual question raised about Marcus Brutus: should he have accepted to have his life spared by the divine Julius when Brutus wanted to kill Caesar? We will examine elsewhere the motivations that led Brutus to kill him. It seems to me however that while on other occasions Brutus behaved as a great man, he made a mistake in this particular instance and did not act according to Stoic principles. In fact he was afraid of the title of king, but there cannot be any other ordering of the state if not under a Just King. Or else he hoped that there could be freedom in a state where great advantages were connected to command and servitude, or he believed that the State could be brought back to the previous constitution while the ancient customs had disappeared. He believed there would be equality

among the citizens and effective and stable laws, and yet he had seen thousands of men fight to decide not whether to be slaves, but who was going to be enslaved. How had he forgotten the laws of nature and the situation of his own city! He believed that once this one was killed no one else would show up with the same intentions, even though there had been a Tarquin after so many kings killed by sword and thunder! He had to accept his life from Caesar, but he was not forced to consider Caesar a father because of this, for only through violence had Caesar acquired the right to do good. One cannot say that Brutus was saved by Caesar who did not kill him, nor that Caesar had acted beneficently but had simply annulled the punishment.[13]

In addition to Seneca's view of the Brutus problem, which coincides entirely with Dante's, two more elements should be noted at this point. First, Seneca's condemnation of Brutus based on Stoic principles does not coincide with a justification of Caesar's position. Indeed, while the events that brought Caesar to absolute power are explained on the basis of historical evolution and necessity, Caesar as an individual is viewed as a violent man: "For only through violence had Caesar acquired the right to do good." Like Brutus, Caesar appears simply as an agent of fate, the one chosen to bring about a new political system. This ultimate "good" does not justify the means used by Caesar, which were, like those of Brutus, violent and based on war. Caesar's victory might explain and vindicate his actions from a point of view that takes into account the meaning of universal history, but certainly does not make him a good or virtuous man in the Stoic sense. After the civil war Caesar did not really pardon Brutus; he just saved him from capital punishment. Like Dante, Seneca separates Caesar's historical persona from the symbolic one. A guilty Caesar may live together with a saintly one, both representing the birth of a new political order.

Second, the sentence in which Seneca says that Brutus was not forced to consider Caesar a father deserves careful examination. In the Brutus-Caesar relationship, "father" will be frequently used after the historical episode is turned into myth. To understand this development the crucial distinction between the historical and the symbolic Julius Caesar should be considered. As a symbol for the Empire, Caesar was thought of as the father of all his subjects, including Brutus. Therefore Brutus' struggle against him, culminating in Brutus' murder of Caesar, was viewed by those sympathetic to the republican ideal as tyrannicide, while those who believed in the Caesarean political project accused Brutus of parricide. In literature concerning political struggles, acts of tyrannicide and parricide often tend to be mixed one with the other, as one person's rule is frequently considered a transferral of the patriarchal family attitude to the political realm. Seneca's sentence, which alludes—even if in an allegorical and abstract sense—to some kind of blood relationship between Brutus and Caesar, captured the imagination of Renaissance writers and influenced their political discussions. It will also play a substantial role in the evolution of the Brutus figure from a moral and political symbol to a tragic character, entangled in the primitive and archaic self-imposed mission of killing both the father and the king.

A philosophical and moral account of the classical authors who fired Dante's imagination in his complex rendition of the Brutus character cannot omit Cicero. There is actually hardly any aspect of Roman history of the first century B.C. in which the able, cunning, rhetorical, articulate, clever, and very ambiguous Cicero does not play his own questionable role. His strong presence evidences the role that the omnipotent art of rhetoric was able to acquire at this high point of Western civilization. In a dialogue dedicated to Brutus, written in 45 B.C. during August, just seven month before the Ides of March of the crucial following year, Cicero expounds on the main philosophical topics of his time. For the purpose of our analysis some comments in books 3 and 4 of Cicero's dialogue *De Finibus,* a dialogue between people who really lived, will be sufficient since these two books contain Cato's summary and Cicero's refutation of the basics of Stoicism. Cicero's objections mainly address the Stoic belief that the ultimate goal of life is morality defined as "life in agreement with virtue" or "life in harmony with nature":

> By what means or at what point did you suddenly discard the body, and all those things which are in accordance with nature but out of our control, and lastly duty itself? My question then is, how comes it that so many things that Nature strongly recommends have been suddenly abandoned by Wisdom? Even if we were not seeking the Chief Good of man but of some living creature that consisted solely of a mind (let us allow ourselves to imagine such a creature, in order to facilitate our discovery of the truth), even so that mind would not accept this End of yours. For such a being would ask for health and freedom from

pain, and would also desire its own preservation, and security for the goods just specified; and it would set up as its end to live according to nature, which means, as I said, to possess either all or most of the most important of the things which are in accordance with nature.[14]

Cicero's criticism of Cato's philosophy relies on materialistic grounds. If Cato believes that virtuous conduct of life must be in accordance with nature and one must therefore accept what nature has to offer, then Cicero is eager to point out that nature's will is not always compatible with human desires. Obviously the context of this passage calls for an understanding of the term "nature" in its widest possible implications, not just as the aggregate of physical events that affect the body and make it feel pleasure or pain. At a very basic level, Cicero says that to pursue a life of virtue and wisdom one needs to be free from the restrictions of need, a condition that nature does not always allow. In its widest connotations, nature here is also intended as history, or the ensemble of those social and political factors that affect individual existence and play a substantial part in our daily life. However, even if we stay with the narrower meaning, it is still possible to point out the substantial differences between the ideas of Cato and those of Cicero. The word "duty" plays an important role in Cicero's refutation of Cato's Stoicism. It indicates that people, in order to improve their own lives as well as the condition of the political body in which they live, must take part in the collective and social aspects of their city's life. In another treatise, the *De Officiis*, written after Caesar's death, Cicero develops even further his practical view of morality and says in a very important passage that the killing of a tyrant is in total agreement with an ethical view of life:

For it often happens, owing to exceptional circumstances, that what is accustomed under ordinary circumstances to be considered morally wrong is found not to be morally wrong. For the sake of illustration, let us assume some particular case that admits of wider application: what more atrocious crime can there be than to kill a fellow-man, and especially an intimate friend? But if anyone kills a tyrant—be he never so intimate a friend—he has not laden his soul with guilt, has he? The Roman People, at all events, are not of that opinion; for all glorious deeds they hold such a one to be the most noble. Has expediency, then, prevailed over moral rectitude? Not at all; moral rectitude has gone hand in hand with expediency.[15]

The closing of this statement, which tries to create a close relationship between expediency and moral rectitude, is representative of Cicero's ideas on morality. In relationship to Dante, Cicero's view of Caesar as a tyrant is not the only aspect that points to a substantial difference between the two. Cicero's morality both in the *De Finibus* and the *De Officiis* is a practical morality, a morality that places expediency at its center. It is a morality of action, which states that the right course is the one that people find more expedient to reach certain results. It is a morality that will receive great attention during the Renaissance, because it describes people as the ultimate judges of their own actions. From Dante's point of view the whole question of morality in the Caesar-Cato issue revolves around a completely different question. Dante not only discusses whether it was right or wrong to kill Caesar, but also whether Cato's suicide, committed in order not to have to yield to Caesar's power, was morally justifiable.

A justification of suicide through Cato's own words appears in book 3 of Cicero's *De Finibus*. Obviously Cicero inserted it there in order to stress the difference between his thinking and that of the Stoic philosopher on this specific topic. Cato's explanation of suicide is a very complex one. Rather than based on a philosophy of action, it is the expression of a philosophy of the appropriate, or moral, act. Since moral good is the ultimate duty of a virtuous person, an appropriate act for Cato is one done in accordance with nature and its circumstances. No moral judgment, either positive or negative, should be made about it. According to Cato, even the prerogative of being able to choose between life and death is included in the realm of the appropriate act: "When a man's circumstances contain a preponderance of things in accordance with nature, it is appropriate for him to remain alive; when he possesses or sees in prospect a majority of the contrary things, it is appropriate for him to depart from life."[16] This explanation shows the sharp distinction between Cato's Stoic, and somewhat mystical, thinking and the pragmatic morality of Cicero, who on other issues was very close to Stoicism. While Cicero believed that the duty of humankind is to create its own destiny and to take action by removing difficulties when things do not follow "in accordance with nature," Cato thought that one of its freedoms included the right to commit suicide in order to anticipate the soul's entry into the afterlife. Despite Dante's great admiration for Cicero, master rhetorician of the Latin language, there is little doubt that he agrees with Cato on this point. That Cato, in canto 1 of the *Purgatory*, represents the first symbol of salvation should leave no doubt about Dante's adherence to the type of Stoicism he professes. Because Cato committed suicide, a sin severely punished in *The Divine Comedy* and one of the worst sins in the Christian view, his presence in the *Purgatory* makes Dante's statement even more meaningful.

The Christian Revolution

To make his point regarding Stoicism and Cato's elevation to a figure that symbolizes martyrdom and anticipates Christ, Dante did not consider the writings of some of the most important Christian philosophers. For example, Augustine, the fifth-century Christian philosopher, doctor of the church, bishop of Hippo, and author of the monumental *The City of God*, sharply criticized the act of suicide even when committed in the belief that it would lead to an afterlife in the presence of God:

> Those who killed themselves are to be admired for the greatness of their souls, not for their judgment. . . . A nobler soul is to be considered one that can tolerate rather than escape a miserable life and that despises with enlightened conscience the judgment of men and especially of the general populace, which is more often than not obfuscated by error. And therefore, if one must consider as an act of courage a man's suicide, one finds that Cleombrotus has this greatness. They say that after having read Plato's book in which immortality of the soul is discussed, he threw himself from a wall and passed from this life to one that he considered better. . . . However the same Plato, whom he had read, could teach him that Socrates' suicide was more an act of courage than of honesty.[17]

The reference to Cleombrotus, an obscure classical figure known only because of his philosophical suicide, leads us, like detectives following an elusive line of thought, from a shadowy character with an improbable name to Cicero. In Cicero's *Tusculan Disputations*, a text unknown to Dante, Cleombrotus is also described as having committed suicide after reading Plato's *Phaedo*. A similar scene is found in Plutarch's *Life of Cato*, where the philosopher is seen as he prepares for death by reading Plato's *Phaedo,* indicating that the Socratic death had become a commonly used literary topic. Just before dying, Cato is described by Plutarch as saying "Now I am my master," signifying that for the Stoic philosopher the process of understanding the self is based on a state of complete indifference to worldly affairs and on the abolition of the fear of death.[18]

Augustine takes a rather different point of view. In describing Cleombrotus' suicide he suggests that a proper reading would have indicated to Cleombrotus that Plato's act is "more an act of courage than of honesty," obviously referring to the last pages of the *Phaedo* where Socrates' suicide in the presence of his crying followers is described as a great act of courage. Augustine is looking to the history and the philosophy of the past in order to find episodes that can confirm his orthodox view of Christianity. Dante's point of view, obviously much more flexible and much more creative, transcends history and philosophy and reaches the realm of the symbolic and the metaphoric in which Cato can serve as an example of salvation. While Augustine's *The City of God* is a philosophical treatise that incorporates and justifies Christian dogma and as such is unable to permit any leeway in its interpretation of such a serious sin as suicide, *The Divine Comedy* conveys its message through more flexible literary and poetic discourse. Augustine's passing reference to Plato to deny the possibility of justifying suicide in whatever circumstance leads him to examine the case of Cato directly. His argument against the Stoic philosopher, although rather weak from a philosophical point of view, is extremely strong when analyzing the meaning of Cato's act:

> What should I say about his gesture? I will say that most of his friends, also men of knowledge, who wisely tried to dissuade him from doing it, judged the gesture as that of a weak man rather than a strong man, because in it one could see not the integrity that opposes dishonor but rather the weakness that cannot oppose adversity. Cato himself proved it with his son. If it was not honorable to live after Caesar's victory, why did he encourage his son to commit such a dishonor, since he advised his son to rely on Caesar's clemency? . . . What should I say, then? That he loved his son so strongly that he wanted him to be saved by Caesar, and yet just as strongly he envied Caesar's glory, as Caesar himself had said, so he couldn't permit himself to be pardoned or, to state it more mildly, he was ashamed to be pardoned?[19]

Unlike literature, history and philosophy do not allow for a free use of historical characters. It is not possible to extract them from their historical situations and to use them, the way Dante uses Cato, as symbolic bridges between two eras. According to Augustine, Cato's suicide, whether based on Plato's ideas on the immortality of the soul or not, proves he is unable to endure the trials and tribulations of life that the good Christian must endure to obtain salvation of the soul.

Just as Dante overlooked Augustine's ideas about Cato, he also did not consider other medieval authors who specifically discussed the Brutus-Cato-Caesar problem or, more generally, the subject of tyrannicide. Among these thinkers at least two, John of Salisbury and Thomas Aquinas, are of crucial importance. While affirming the predominance of church government over political power, the twelfth-century philosopher John of Salisbury expressed no sympathy for tyranny and justified tyrannicide on many grounds. His treatise, the *Polycraticus,* is one of the classics of early modern political science and its principles had an influence on the political thinking of the Renaissance. The legacy of the *Polycraticus* was especially felt in one of the most important early fifteenth-century political treatises, Coluccio Salutati's *De Tyranno.* John of Salisbury is careful to distinguish between the ruler—also called *Princeps* (Prince), which he sees as personifying the best form of government—and the tyrant. With this difference having been delineated—a difficult distinction to make and one to which Coluccio Salutati would dedicate a major part of his treatise—John of Salisbury goes on to say that tyrannicide is not only a necessity but the good citizen's duty: "The Prince is the image of God, and must be loved, revered and admired; the tyrant is the image of depravity, and first of all he must be killed. The origin of tyranny is injustice, and from a diseased root breeds evils and sickness, and infects the tree. . . ."[20] However, when specifically discussing Caesar, John of Salisbury appears to be in a more difficult position. He seems to be divided in his thinking by the need to respect the myth of Caesar as the symbol of the Roman Empire while being forced by coherence in his reasoning to recognize that Caesar had indeed abolished all Roman republican liberties and subjected the state to his rule:

> However, because he occupied the Republic with arms, he was considered a tyrant, and when the majority of the senators were in agreement, they took up their knives and he was killed in the Capitol. But even in this circumstance he did not lose his

integrity. When in fact he realized that they were after him with knives, he wrapped his head in his toga and, at the same time, held his left hand to his chest so that he would fall more honestly.[21]

Thomas Aquinas' ideas on tyranny do not drastically differ from those of John of Salisbury. Aquinas believes that tyranny represents a negative condition for the state. On the other hand, he believes that tyranny is very often the natural outcome of a degenerative process that takes place in the republican order, sometimes called the government of the many. Aquinas, again like John of Salisbury, trusts that the rule of one is the best form of government because it can prevent the degeneration into tyranny. In the presence of tyranny, however, Aquinas calls for collective action to bring it down. The act of one or a few individuals cannot prevent the would-be tyrant from becoming a tyrant or bring down the tyrant who is already in power. Unlike John of Salisbury, Aquinas seems convinced that the action against Caesar was not a collective one, but a secret plot conducted by Brutus. Aquinas wholeheartedly trusted in the political process and believed that whatever action was to be taken had to be taken within a clearly established framework of rules of behavior: "Therefore it is clear that against the tyrant's cruelty one must proceed not through individual decision but through public authority. And, in the first place, if it is up to a collective body to nominate a king according to law, the same collective body can bring him down or limit his power, if he tragically abuses his power."[22]

This statement, along with another one in which he states that Caesar became a tyrant ("Caesar . . . obtained for himself power and monarchy, and turned politics into despotism, which is tyranny"[23]) indicates quite clearly that, even more than John of Salisbury, Thomas Aquinas does not bow to the Caesarean myth.

Augustine, John of Salisbury, and Thomas Aquinas are Christian thinkers who interpret history, both pre-Christian and Christian, in a philosophical way. Their intention is to discover what the past has to tell us about the present and to show how the past is, in essence, just a preparation for the Christian world and an anticipation of its moral message. Given this framework these philosophers' teachings are written very clearly and do not contain the multi-levels of meaning that are the unique prerogatives of poetry and literature. While deeply steeped in classical and Christian history and philosophy, Dante's *Divine Comedy* belongs to a different literary genre, a genre that the poet himself created. It is not a political or a moral treatise. It does not establish rules of behavior. It is more than anything else a poetic analysis of how people make decisions, of what compels action or non-action. Through allegory and examples *The Divine Comedy* also discusses the conditions under which our actions can be subjected to moral judgment and when human activity, even if morally deplorable, can be considered guiltless. Dante does not believe in universal rules that can be regularly applied to all similar cases and that can be equally subjected to the same moral judgment. Two identical actions can be motivated by very different reasons. The poet's focus is on the motivation, the impulse that has its origin in the soul. Just as he does not believe in absolute good and evil, Dante thinks that it is impossible to create an inventory of the various types of human actions. However, he strongly believes that there are, and should be, limitations to people's ability to act as they wish. Life should be considered a passing stage in a timeless existence, to be used as a preparation for eternal life.

Dante bases his condemnation of Brutus and the interpretation of Caesar as a historical character symbolizing the secular aspect of God's universe on this principle. Although Caesar may have committed crimes, Dante considers his revolution a part of God's design, a necessary passage on the way to a better world. Moreover, and on this point Dante seems to follow Thomas Aquinas, he believes that it is not the individual's responsibility to stop the fulfillment of destiny.

Dante the Ancient and Dante the Modern: History and Allegory

The Renaissance's perplexities over Dante's treatment of Cato, Brutus, and Caesar are quite easy to understand. When compared with his medieval predecessors such as Augustine, John of Salisbury, and Thomas Aquinas, Dante appears unique and his adherence to Stoicism nearly univocal. As Dante emerges as the most "Roman" or the last "Roman" of medieval authors, an image of the Renaissance takes shape that induces us to believe that the revival of classical culture was precisely what its name indicates. It was the first modern neo-classical movement through which a romantic infatuation for antiquity tried to revive the formal, rather than the authentic, aspects of a world and an era that, by general consensus, were believed to have exhausted their historical cycle.

Most of the historical figures, both on the side of the actors and on the side of the authors, involved in the Brutus story are united by a common destiny in the act of suicide. Lucan and Seneca both ended their own lives in A.D. 65 when their participation in Piso's plot against the emperor Nero was discovered. Cato, as is well known, killed himself in 46 B.C. after the defeat of the Pompeian party. Brutus and Cassius killed themselves at Philippi. Only Caesar and Cicero were killed by someone else's hand—Caesar by Brutus, and Cicero by Anthony's men. So the question naturally arises: why did Dante focus so much of his interest and thoughts concerning politics and morality on a group of men who either killed others or killed themselves, or, as in the case of Brutus, first killed another and then himself?

The question, while puzzling on the surface, is rather easy to answer. First, all these men, whether they were the historical characters involved in the political events of Roman history preceding and immediately following the death of Caesar or the poets and writers who left accounts of those events, played a central role in the evolution of the Republic to the Empire. Dante believed this evolution was one of the pivotal and most meaningful points in universal history, particularly because the political order emerged during the period when Christ was alive. Second, death played a central role in Dante's thinking. He thought of death as the goal of existence; *The Divine Comedy* is often interpreted as a literary experience intended by its author to function as a revelation of the Christian meaning of death. If life has a meaning, Dante believed, its meaning is to be found in the meaning of death. By concentrating his attention and his literary interest on those classical authors whose philosophical or historical lives were centered around the theme of death, Dante was obviously looking for examples from the past that could inspire him in his exploration. In his earlier work the *Convivio* Dante placed Seneca, the Roman philosopher of death, on the same level with Socrates, the Greek philosopher who chose to die rather than retract his ideas.[24]

Dante's choice of Cato as the primary symbol of salvation needs, however, another word of explanation. Quite often scholars and writers who have approached this subject in an attempt to understand how, in Dante's rather orderly and structured geography of sin, a pagan and a suicide could function as the symbol of Christian salvation, have concluded their investigations without an answer. But is Cato a mystery for Dante? Not really. Dante's ideas and generally very negative views about suicide do not actually involve the act itself but rather focus on the process through which most suicides decide to take their own life. The character Dante uses to describe the guilty suicide is Pier della Vigna, punished in the *Inferno* for reasons that appear very clear from the conversation that Dante and Pier della Vigna have in the thirteenth canto. Pier della Vigna explains that he was the chief confidant and the most cherished advisor of the emperor Frederick II, whose court he attended. In explaining his position in *The Divine Comedy*, he says that he "held both keys of Frederick's heart" and that he "kept his counsel and let few men through."[25] For reasons unknown to us, Pier della Vigna fell into the emperor's disgrace, so he was imprisoned and blinded. He then took his life. Dante's condemnation is clearly expressed through Pier della Vigna's own fictional words in the same canto:

> So, in a scornful spirit of disgust,
> And thinking to escape from scorn by death,
> To my just self I made myself injust.[26]

Pier della Vigna committed suicide to escape the shame of being unjustly considered a traitor, which he forcefully says he was not ("To my just self . . . "). He committed suicide to punish himself and to redress a sin that he was only guilty of in others' eyes, not to save the integrity of his own guiltless "self," as was the case with Cato. Pier della Vigna's death is an escape from the self, while Cato's is a reunification with it. Cato's unwillingness to participate in the struggle opposing Caesar to Pompeius and his choice of death for the freedom that others hoped to find in the restoration of the republican order were important to Dante. This point is beautifully made in the first canto of the *Purgatory* when Virgil, who accompanies Dante on his journey, in answering one of Cato's questions explains how Dante, a pilgrim journeying through the afterworld who is coming from hell, is able to enter the universe of the saved:

> "Not my power, but Heaven's design
> Brought me; a lady stopped from bliss to pray
> My aid and escort for this charge of mine;
>
> But since it is thy will I should display
> More fully how it stands now with our case,
> What will could be in me to say thee nay?

This man has not yet seen his term of days,
Yet in his crazy wickedness he drew
So near to it, he had but short breathing-space.

So, as I said, I was dispatched to do
My utmost for his rescue; nor appeared
Any good way save this I've set me to.

I've shown him Hell with all its guilty herd,
And mean to show him next the souls who dwell
Making purgation here beneath thy ward.

How I have brought him through, 'twere long to tell;
Power from on high helps me to guide his feet
To thee, to see and hear and mark thee well.

Be gracious to his coming, I entreat;
'Tis liberty he seeks—how dear a thing
That is, they know who gave their lives for it;

Thou know'st; for thee this passion drew death's sting
In Utica, where thou didst doff the weed
Which at the Doom shall shine so glistering."[27]

The second important reason that Dante chose Cato to represent salvation is because of the role Cato played in the political events that occurred while the imperial system was developing as the new political system for Rome. In this respect Cato is indirectly used as an explanation for Brutus' punishment. In fact, despite his closeness to Cato and his adherence to Stoic philosophy, Brutus decided to take an active part in the political struggle with the hope of reviving a historically obsolete political system. Precisely because he was so close to Brutus and a witness to Brutus' determination in his fight against Caesar, Cato functions also as the symbolic witness of an evil act, the guiltless man who is forced to take his own life because everything around him is polluted with guilt. Like Socrates before him and Christ after him, Cato is to Dante the witness and the martyr, two actions not distinguished in the Greek verb *marturomai*, from which both words are derived. Cato's death, a death that he freely chose while other options were available, was a severe testament to the evils of his times. His death is very similar to the later deaths of the Christian martyrs, mystics who put their ideas and faith before their lives.

While Dante uses Cato symbolically, he treats Brutus and Cassius in their literal and historical contexts. Their story, unlike that of Ulysses, has not been changed, and they are faithfully portrayed in *The Divine Comedy* according to the historical sources that would have been available to Dante. Obviously the assumption can be made, and indeed is often made, that if Dante had known the whole story about Brutus he might have sympathized with him. But this is, precisely, an assumption. On the other hand, even with more historical information about Brutus, Dante could have chosen to use him symbolically as the parricide and to punish him in hell just the same. This final possibility leads us to two other conceivable conclusions from a theoretical point of view. First, symbolism is often an easy way around historical evidence, and second, it is easier to appear historically accurate when few or no historical sources are available to keep an author in check!

It is indeed interesting to speculate on how Dante would have treated the Brutus figure had he been familiar with the work of other historians, especially Plutarch's biography of Brutus. Plutarch gives Brutus psychological depth, showing a character torn by moral dilemmas who reaches the decision to kill Caesar with great difficulty. Although this decision results from deep meditation and profound thinking, it is still the same decision. Dante probably would not have changed his portrayal of the character even if he had read in Plutarch about the complexity of Brutus' moral stance. At best, Dante would have adopted a more symbolic treatment of Brutus. The poet's historical depiction of Brutus is simply by chance; had Dante known more about Brutus, he would have nevertheless condemned him to hell, justifying the decision from an allegorical and symbolic point of view. In Brutus Dante wanted the killer of the founder of the Empire. The available historical reports that favored this interpretation were just a stroke of luck. Had Plutarch been available, Brutus would have been turned into a symbol, like Cato and Caesar.

Caesar appears in Dante as an allegorical figure, representing all Roman emperors and the imperial institution itself. In his political treatise *De Monarchia*, in which Dante discusses the role of the emperor vis-à-vis the church, this interpretation appears very clearly:

> I believe that I have now reached the goal I was aiming at. In fact we have found the true solution to the three problems

regarding whether the role of the monarch is necessary to the good of the world, whether the Roman people rightfully acquired the Empire, and whether the Monarch's authority comes directly from God or from someone else. The true solution to the last problem must not be misunderstood in the sense that the Roman Prince should not in any way be subjected to the Roman Pontiff, since the terrestrial happiness is in some way guided by eternal happiness. Caesar must therefore relate to Peter with the same kind of respect that the firstborn son owes his father. So that, enlightened by the grace and the vision of the Father, he may irradiate them more effectively throughout the world in which he has been placed as a guide by Him who alone is the guide of all spiritual and temporal things.[28]

Another confirmation of Dante's employment of Caesar as an allegorical figure comes from knowing that the poet had read in Cicero and Seneca about Caesar's crimes. However, that did not change the role that Caesar plays in the general design of *The Divine Comedy*, where he stands as the terrestrial counterpart to Peter, the successor of Christ.

During the Renaissance the combination of Caesar as a symbol of the Empire and as an actual historical figure will be criticized and the two aspects will again be separated. This separation, as well as the discovery of more historical sources describing in greater depth Brutus' moral dilemmas, will produce a criticism of Dante's interpretation of the Brutus-Caesar issue aimed at underscoring the contrast between image and reality, history, philosophy and allegory, nature and nature's model. In the discussion of these often opposed topics the Renaissance's passion for rhetoric will play itself out.

Finally, Dante's treatment of Brutus and Cato, and tangentially his evaluation of Caesar, can also be read as Dante's evaluation of the ancient world. Unlike most of the authors of the Middle Ages and of later times, perhaps even to the Enlightenment, Dante had a keen interest in classical history. Although he saw himself as the product of postclassical times and described his age as a new age permeated by the Christian spirit, Dante was interested in interpreting the classical world as a sort of preparation for the Christian world. Dante thought of the classical world as a world in which, Christianity not yet having revealed itself, the reality of the new age to come was disguised under obscure and deceiving symbols. According to him it was a world in which providence had not yet made its goal known to humankind; therefore it was more difficult for humankind to identify the right course to follow. Dante considers Brutus a typical figure of the classical world. Whether the poet's understanding of the killer of Caesar was limited and necessarily narrowed by the lack of some historical sources, such as Plutarch's, for Dante Brutus remains exemplary of the classical, centripetal turn of mind. Brutus, trying to turn the clock of history backward, saw perfection in the past and had no faith in the possibilities of the future. Cato, on the contrary, in choosing between a wrongful life and an afterlife full of possibilities, ended up favoring the latter. In comparing Dante with Augustine one cannot help but conclude that Dante allowed greater freedom to the powers of human vision and ideals. For him, when properly justified, even suicide becomes a moral possibility.

Conclusion

In a letter to Cicero, dated 15 May 43 B.C., Brutus wrote:

> While Caesar was living and before accomplishing my act, I was not really myself, nor could I feel comfortable in exile in any part of the world where I would continue to hate servitude and abjection as the worst evils. And is it not to succumb to the same darkness when one asks for clemency for those who fought for liberty and tried to fight tyranny from him who chose the name of tyrant? In the Greek cities the sons of tyrants followed the same fate as their fathers when they were killed.[29]

Dante probably did not know of this letter. Familiarity with it might have added fuel to his bias against Brutus, since the letter confirms in Brutus' own words all of Dante's reasons for his punishment. Brutus is trying to convince Cicero here not to ask Octavius, Caesar's successor, to forgive and save the lives of those who fought against Caesar. Doesn't Octavius, Brutus asks, deserve death just like Caesar did? Isn't it a rule of Greek tragedy that the sons of tyrants, whether biological sons or successors, encounter the same fate as their fathers? The solution, Brutus says, is to kill Octavius too. Until I killed Caesar, Brutus tells Cicero, "I was not really myself," indirectly indicating that Caesar, by pardoning him after the civil war, forced Brutus into a position of subjection and compelled him to believe that he owed his life to Caesar. Not until this debt and this tie—

almost an Oedipal tie—was abolished on the Ides of March, was Brutus able to feel like a whole, free person. Through the killing, by annihilating the man who had saved his life and had later made himself the sole ruler of Rome, Brutus was able to feel free, both in a political and moral sense. Brutus mentions the rules of Greek tragedy and demonstrates he is aware of tragedy's fatal mechanism, but does not mention the possibility that his own act may soon encounter reciprocation. However, according to the very rules of the mechanism that Brutus wants to serve as an example for political practice, by killing Caesar he has set in motion the course of events that will lead to his own tragic demise. Precisely because he is unable to understand this pattern, because he unconsciously follows pre-established models of behavior, Dante deems Brutus worthy of only the lowest place in hell. Cato's case is quite different. In Dante's view Cato chose the only possible ethical course of action, given the conditions in which he was living.

Dante's decision to use Cato, despite his suicide, as the symbol of salvation could ultimately contain an element of autobiographical identification. Dante, aside from being the poet and author of *The Divine Comedy*, is also its main character and could probably see himself as a modern, Christian version of Cato, who is also looking for eternal salvation. Like Cato, Dante was actively involved in the political events of Florence, the native city from which he was finally exiled. With the failure of his political ideals when he was banned from the city, Dante was, like Cato, a man without a land who needed to come to terms with his destiny. He had lost his civic role and was condemned to a life of pilgrimage from one city to the other in search of protection and peace. In *Paradise*, not far from the ultimate revelation of God, Dante meets with his ancestor Cacciaguida who in a long speech reveals to him the realities of his plight:

As, through his stepdame's treacherous lust unkind,
Hippolytus from Athens had to go,
So thou must needs leave Florence town behind;

So willed, it is so planned, and soon will so
Be done by him who sits and plots that same,
Where Christ is daily huckstered to and fro.

The injured side will bear the common blame
As ever; but the day of reckoning,
By truth appointed, shall the truth proclaim.

Thou shalt abandon each and every thing
Most dear to thee: that shaft's the first that e'er
The bow of exile looses from the string;

Thou shalt by sharp experience be aware
How salt the bread of strangers is, how hard
The up and down of someone else's stair;

And heaviest on thy shoulders afterward
Shall the companions of thy ruin weigh,
All with one brush of vice and violence tarred;

For with a savage fury they play
The ingrate, and defame thee; yet anon
Not thou shalt feel thy forehead burn, but they—

Fools all, and proved so by their goings-on;
Well shall it be for thee to have preferred
Making a party of thyself alone.[30]

Cacciaguida's prophecy that announces to Dante that he will be forced out of his city contains the advice to make "a party of thyself alone," to become his own master, alone in a corrupted and guilty world. A quintessentially Stoic message, it is similar to Cato's self-consciousness before his suicide, as described in Lucan and in Plutarch, only with a difference: Cato did not have a Christian revelation that could indicate to him the proper course to follow after destiny had played out its cards. Dante did. For Cato the only possible choice was suicide. For Dante it was to prepare for eternal life in his search for God's revelation. Both conditions—faithful to Stoic philosophy—treat death as the ultimate deliverance from the confinements of human existence. Given the different cultural conditions in which Cato and Dante lived, it is as if they both made the same decision.

2

Brutus Carries Out His Destiny

The Renaissance Transformation

Dante is commonly regarded as a medieval author in the history of Italian literature. On the Brutus-Cato-Caesar issue Dante appears medieval only on the surface; even his defense of Caesar, a Caesar seen not only as the historical figure but also as the symbol for the Empire, is not absolutely medieval.

The notion that the coming of the Empire was within destiny's design, willed by forces outside of mortal control, was a classical idea that later became medieval. Virgil clearly expressed this idea in his celebrated *Fourth Eclogue*, and Dante indeed refers to Virgil in *On Monarchy* and in *Purgatory*.[1] The Christians, and Dante with them, may well have added the figure of a revealed God to the more obscure concept of destiny used by the classics, but the idea of a universal Empire certainly does not identify the poet in strictly medieval terms. As we saw in the preceding chapter, Dante's defense of Cato, the suicide, appears almost antimedieval, and certainly nondogmatic, and should be read as a strong affirmation of classical morality. The same can be said of Brutus, whose figure Dante interpreted on the basis of the few sources available to him.

Unfortunately our understanding of Dante the poet, and even more so of Dante the philosopher and the religious man, is still largely influenced by traditional literary criticism based on historicism and historical determinism. Such criticism views works of art and their creators exclusively as the necessary products of their times, as if an overwhelming and all-encompassing cultural climate was able to dictate the most secret and personal sources of creativity. Little allowance is usually made for those independent artists and thinkers, ingenious and unique minds, who are able to leave their mark even when the spirit of the times should guide them otherwise. A sad legacy of romantic historicism compels us to believe that art always imitates life, that the picture is always the copy of nature, and never considers that the opposite, at least potentially, could also be true.

The possibility that the works of Dante and all of the major artists of the Western tradition shaped a great part of what came after them is a hypothesis that deserves serious consideration. It is not such an unusual hypothesis if we think of postmedieval Western culture—from the Renaissance to modern times—as a culture that has increasingly valued invention over experience and experiment over tradition. During the Renaissance, which Dante anticipates, the Western world learned the wider importance of the image over the object, of the idea over the fact. One of the most celebrated novels of the modern era, Cervantes' *Don Quixote* narrates the story of a man who wants to act out the deeds narrated in other novels he has read. Cervantes describes his hero as having lost his mind through the power of sheer infatuation. On the other hand, during the course of the novel the reader learns that Don Quixote has an enviable amount of common sense that always allows him to emerge somewhat victorious from the incredible situations in which he gets involved. The balance between apparent madness and actual common sense, one of the enduring features of the novel, is probably the core of Cervantes' message: ideas are no longer separable from reality. Modern reality is but a construction of the individual and of the collective mind.

A careful consideration of the way in which Dante views the figures of Brutus, Caesar, and Cato reveals that his treatment is hardly medieval. The major difference between Dante and the Humanists in their treatment of Brutus involves the theme of the Empire. One reason that the Humanists appeared to be more sympathetic to Brutus than Dante was because the ideal of a universal Empire incarnated in the Dantesque figure of Caesar was no longer upheld as a truth that could not be questioned. The Renaissance was, after all, the period of the independent city-states, of the rebirth of ancient republican values, and most of all, the period during which the modern idea of the state was slowly taking shape. This political process and philosophical evolution stimulated substantial changes, if not radical reversals, in cultural interests.

During this process the Brutus character will emerge from Dante's dramatic lines of moral and religious damnation and will be transferred to the pages of the Humanists with a more rounded and individual persona. Without losing the power of the symbol, he will acquire the frailty of a human being. In this transformation he will become more of a political figure and less of a moral one, perhaps anticipating Machiavelli's separation of politics from ethics, and leaves behind the image of the Roman citizen infatuated with Stoic philosophy. His actions will no longer be considered illustrative of a way of life repudiated by Dante as brutal and primitive, and he will be seen more and more as a modern warrior, the man of action who tries to preserve and protect the freedom and greatness of his city.

The evolution from one portrayal to the other will not be a smooth one, primarily because it will inevitably necessitate sharp criticism of Dante's position, not an easy task, especially in the city of Dante's birth. Therefore, whenever the issue of Brutus arises along with the question of vindicating his honor, the art of rhetoric and ingenious speech, accompanied more often than not by hairsplitting and Byzantine distinctions, will be the method of reconciling Dante's poetic excellence and Brutus' political vision.

Never faithful friends, literature and politics will find great friction in the Dante-Brutus opposition of the Renaissance. A resolution of this incompatibility will be attempted by the art of rhetoric, that special craft in the usage of words that seems to have been created in the name of compromise between the world of ideas and ideals and the world of expediency. Most of the Renaissance rhetorical treatises dealing, exclusively or in part, with Brutus depict a double Brutus, one torn between morality and practicality, divided between what is good and what is expedient. The rediscovery of Plutarch's biography of Brutus at the beginning of the fifteenth century adds fuel to this kind of double interpretative standard and will help create the myth of Brutus as the modern man, torn between two opposite alternatives. This Brutus will walk out of the written page, like a character of Pirandello, and assume the life and the human depth that were not allowed to him in the rhetorical diatribes of the Humanist treatises. The Brutus of those treatises will inflame the hearts and souls of the many new breathing, living Brutuses, the republican and populist freedom fighters well known to Italian Renaissance courts, the new Brutuses who found in the Roman Brutus the great model for political virtue. Contradictions are harder to reconcile in life than they are on paper. Cicero and his perfect art are not always at hand when personal hatred, combined with political differences, opens the door to a feud for power. The Renaissance Brutuses were living proof that life follows art and not vice versa.

Tyrannicide acquired an unprecedented popularity during the Renaissance.[2] Whenever and wherever a *signore* overstepped the boundaries of power consigned to him by tradition, immediately one or more conspirators, almost without exception claiming to be the political inheritors of Brutus' legacy, thought it was their duty towards their city and the nobility of their souls to do away with the new Caesar.

It would be a mistake to claim that Dante was the only author responsible for the transmission of the Brutus myth to the modern world. The Renaissance's passion for the classics, the conviction that in the classics one could find all examples of political and moral virtue, also played a major role. However, Dante's position on Brutus added another dimension to the Brutus character. If the classical Brutus was a man torn between difficult choices—whether to kill Caesar and save the Republic or let Caesar live because Caesar had saved his life—Dante's Brutus is judged in the name of a higher moral value. With Dante the question is no longer whether or not to kill Caesar and which one of the two choices is the correct one, but what is the meaning of human action and of individual decisions? Can one individual, through free will, change the course of history? Is it right for a single self-appointed person to judge the political body and, if deemed necessary, to act in order to change its course? Dante answered these questions with a very clear "no." The Renaissance, divided like Brutus between an ideal view of human events and a practical one, questioned Dante's point of view. In this process of questioning—a questioning and a probing never resulting in a clear solution— Brutus, after taking on life in the flesh and blood of the Brutuses of Renaissance history, was transformed into a tragic figure. The Renaissance expressed itself in its representation of the Brutus figure, as in all its other artistic and cultural manifestations, as divided between an ideal view of the world and a concrete and practical one. While it tried to make reality adhere to an ideal view, the Renaissance realized the impossibility of bridging this gap.

Following the 1537 assassination of Alessandro de' Medici by the "new Brutus," Lorenzino de' Medici, Michelangelo celebrated the event by sculpting a bust of Brutus now preserved in the Bargello Museum in Florence. In the statue the artist idealized the liberator and the freedom fighter who strives to affirm with his actions the importance of human dignity against a despotic ruler. Following this initial enthusiasm for the heroic deed, Michelangelo is portrayed in a dialogue by Donato Giannotti, written in the typical Renaissance form, on Dante's treatment of Brutus.[3] In this dialogue Michelangelo's initial enthusiasm for Lorenzino's act is largely attenuated by a complex philosophical meditation that involves the meaning of human action and the role of individual responsibility. Does the act of killing the tyrant, of eliminating an evil, necessarily bring about a better situation? Or can an evil like tyranny be a way through which destiny improves, in due course, the condition of the state? These questions, at once political, moral, and philosophical, are the questions of Renaissance literature. They will be repeated over and over again, in reference to Brutus and, more generally, in discussions concerning the relationship between the individual and society.

The mind of Renaissance Italy, and especially of Renaissance Florence, was shaped by the concourse of different cultural traditions, the Greek, the Roman, the medieval and the Dantesque. These currents were brought together in the intellectual arena of the fourteenth century and each contributed its own specific point of view to what it means to be human. Political events also played an important role. The myth of Roman republicanism, which at least in the beginning was the guiding principle for the Italian city-state, was constantly threatened by attempts to establish a single ruler. The intellectual debate was therefore dramatized and enriched by matters of political expediency. Could Brutus' republican ideal be held as the universal political model, or did the reign of one ruler also have its positive aspects, such as an assurance of order and internal peace? Should ideals be overlooked when the security of the state is at risk?

The debate between the ideal and the practical is especially clear in the life and the works of Machiavelli. In *The Prince*, often considered a tragic work both in content and in structure,[4] the populist and republican Machiavelli calls for a powerful prince to resolve in an orderly fashion the many Italian divisions and internal fights. According to Machiavelli, the state of emergency justifies whatever means the prince believes most effective to bring back order. Machiavelli in fact used this work to reveal a theory of politics totally contrary to his ideals and beliefs, and from this point of view *The Prince* is characteristic of the entire cultural mood of the late Renaissance, torn as it also was by religious and moral dilemmas. Again the Brutus figure, through his own evolution, is symptomatic of the more general cultural evolution. Revived in Dante's poem and in the literature of his followers, taking on life in the "new Brutuses," and finally returning into the world of fiction in tragic theatre, Brutus covers the entire Renaissance development, beginning with *The Divine Comedy* and culminating in Shakespeare's *Julius Caesar* and *Hamlet*.

Renaissance tragedy, from the initial late sixteenth-century Italian attempts to its climax in Shakespeare, expresses a deep sense of uncertainty about the individual's ability to shape personal destiny. The essence of pre-Shakespearean and Shakespearean tragedy could be defined as representing the clash between action and thought: action is the process of carrying out what is morally dictated by traditional cultural values and thought is the intellectual reflection that constantly questions the worth of such values. It will become clear throughout this chapter that this clash was also the essence of the Renaissance's interest in Brutus before he was turned into a tragic character.

A number of early Italian, French, and English tragedies dealt with the figure of Brutus, and Brutus is, of course, the central character in Shakespeare's *Julius Caesar*. To trace the link connecting the pre-tragic Brutus to the tragic one, one must follow Renaissance writings sequentially and study the cultural process that led Brutus to become a figure of such preeminent importance. By following this path we will discover an increasingly complex Brutus, a historical figure turned into a myth intended to mirror some of the most crucial moral, philosophical, and psychological issues of the times. An important cultural chapter in the history of the modern age and in the psychological development of modern humanity can be outlined through Brutus. Between Dante's damned Brutus and Shakespeare's "man within himself at war" lies the history of the birth of modern tragic feeling.

Petrarch and Boccaccio as Interpreters of Brutus

A series of comments made by Petrarch and Boccaccio on the Brutus figure represent a clear evolution from Dante's point of view. Petrarch's ideas about the killing of Caesar and the passions that motivated it are found, among other places, in a letter to the Signore of Padova, Francesco da Carrara.[5] The intent of the letter is to praise its addressee for his virtuous conduct as the ruler of his city. As is common in Humanist writings, the basis for the praise is provided by comparing da Carrara's deeds with those of some classical rulers; obviously Julius Caesar could not be excluded. While Petrarch's ideas on the killing of Caesar agree substantially with those of Dante, this letter contains some interesting comments on Cicero's changing attitudes toward the figure of Caesar. In this respect Petrarch treats absolute power quite differently from Dante, as it appears not to be justified on ideological or religious grounds. Rather, for Petrarch the issue of absolute power does not seem to be a moral one as much as a practical one, its existence being justified by the public support it is able to command:

> As far as praising others is concerned, in fact, I dislike both adulation and, even more so, the inconsistencies of him who adulates. There are in fact people who praise those not worthy, and others who with absolute lack of concern criticize those whom they have praised, which is a thing truly dishonest and despicable. It is a sin of which Cicero was guilty, so that while I love him and prefer him above all writers, as far as this sin is concerned, I almost hate him. Without talking of others, he praises Julius Caesar with such words that he almost seems to burden him, and after that he covers him with insults and maledictions. Read his letters to his brother Quintus: They speak of Caesar with respect and friendship. Now look at his letters to Atticus: the first one is ambiguous, in the last one you will find hideous and inflamed statments. Then read the speeches that he delivered before the very same Caesar or, with him present, before the Senate: you will find in them such great praise for Caesar that they will not seem to be addressed to a mortal nor uttered by a mortal mind. Keep reading: read the *De Officiis* and the *Philippics*: You will find in them a hatred not less powerful than the former love, and insults not inferior to the former praises; what disgusts me more in so much inconsistency is that all the praises were said when he was alive and all the insults when he was dead. I would have better understood his inconsistency if he had insulted him while he was alive and praised him after his death. Death, in fact, usually extinguishes or mitigates envy and hatred.[6]

In this letter, Petrarch does not defend tyranny or monarchical power. His ideas about these issues are quite complex, ranging from an accusation in *Africa* concerning Caesar's lust for absolute power to an understanding of the "medieval concept of Universal Monarchy" in the *De Gestis Caesaris*.[7] The letter to Francesco da Carrara is of special interest not because it reveals Petrarch's ideas about monarchy, but because the issue of power is treated mainly from a psychological point of view, a clear shift from Dante's position. In Petrarch the basis for power rests on the ability of the ruler to find and maintain popular support, not on any predetermined philosophical assumption. Petrarch is therefore moving toward a more pragmatic view of power and assumes, by implication, that one of power's major justifications is the ruler's ability to hold it. This is clearly not a Machiavellian statement as it does not openly assert the prince's right to resort to all possible means to keep his rule, but it certainly asserts the paramount importance, in matters concerning the state, of the ruler's ability to keep his position.

In examining the development of the Brutus figure, Petrarch's position is even more revealing. In his discussion of power, the poet gives great importance to the psychological dynamics between the ruler and the ruled when the ruler attempts to establish absolute power. And in another section of the letter in which Petrarch discusses whether it is better for the absolute ruler to be loved or hated by his subjects, the focus of the discussion shifts from a strictly political mood to a tragic one. The discussion revolves around a speech by Atreus, the mythical king of Mycene who, because of his crimes, was inflicted with a fateful and ominous curse against his family. In discussing this speech, ("Let them hate me, as long as they fear me")—which the author believes was written by Euripides but is by the Latin poet Accius[8]—Petrarch establishes that the prince's ability to maintain power depends largely on his individual political talents and on his relationship with his subjects. While on one hand he asserts that the prince who relies exclusively on fear as a means of maintaining power is doomed, on the other, using Caesar as an example, Petrarch is unable to prove that by being generous and gracious toward his subjects the ruler can protect himself from hatred, envy, and their destructive consequences. Speaking of Caesar, he adds:

> In fact, aside from his lust for glory and power, a lust quite excessive in him, he did his best to be loved rather than feared, at times demonstrating his magnanimity and clemency, and at other times his great generosity, to such a degree that, after all the victories and the supreme command he obtained, he wanted no other privilege but that of government, as is proven by many records. He was moreover so inclined to grant pardons that the predictable Cicero said that Caesar forgot nothing aside from

offenses. To pardon offenses is a noble revenge, but even more noble is to forget them—and Caesar accomplished this to such an extent that even he who was first his friend and then his enemy acknowledged this quality as his most important one. In conclusion: not to speak of his other virtues, he was richer in this one than anybody else, even if he did not profit from it as he should have. He was in fact killed precisely by those whom he had elevated to the highest honors and whom he had pardoned for former enmities and offenses, renouncing his rights as the winner.[9]

Why was Caesar killed by Brutus and the other conspirators? In a complex discussion of the emotional mechanism that brought Caesar to his death, Petrarch studies the interplay of several elements: hatred, envy, and destiny. There is little doubt in Petrarch's mind that Caesar was a great leader, a man of vision who was able to see the direction of history before anyone else. His ability to anticipate events prompted him to propose himself as the destined ruler. In turn, such confidence and vision was cause for envy and hatred, even on the part of his former friends and protégés: "In such circumstances one must ask why he attracted so much hatred, because in the plot against him there was hatred. I see no other reason outside of his lofty and self-conscious sense of superiority which led him to elevate himself too much above the traditional ways. . . ."[10]

Ironically, Petrarch attributes the causes of Caesar's fall to his ability to anticipate historical events. But Petrarch's crucial analysis of power and its preservation originates precisely from this notion and from the insight that even someone superior like Caesar could not escape the curse of hatred and envy. If hatred is so pervasive in the political body, if envy casts jealous subjects against the good prince, how does the good prince preserve his power? What is the antidote to envy? Speaking in general terms and not specifically about Caesar, Petrarch says that love—a love similar to Dante's universal love—is the antidote to envy and to the political strife it causes. The real loving prince, the one who will love his subjects truly and honestly, will be loved in turn by them, thus becoming legitimately "the father of the state," without risk of being overthrown.[11] The power of love is all-encompassing, according to Petrarch; its reach knows no boundaries.

This final assumption clearly contradicts what Petrarch had stated previously and makes his discussion of Caesar's assassination rather inconclusive. Shortly after lauding his generosity and willingness to forget and pardon offenses, Petrarch had in fact attributed Caesar's fall to others' envy of his incomparable vision. Petrarch does not doubt that individuals of outstanding qualities and unusual abilities easily become the objects of hatred and of envy. He then adds that love is the solution to the problem, but does not elaborate on the matter aside from stating, rather enigmatically, that the prince should turn himself into "the father of the state." By doing this Petrarch seems to want to bring a complex discussion to a simple conclusion. Had he known anything about Greek tragedy and the consequences of combining the affairs of the family with those of the state, he would not have used the image of "father of the state" even metaphorically. It is a dangerous metaphor, one that may also have played a role in setting Brutus against Caesar. Caesar was, in fact, the lover of Brutus' mother, and Brutus' father died when Brutus was very young. Was Brutus confused about his paternity? Did Petrarch's and the later Humanists' inclination to identify the prince with "the father of the state," eventually combined with Greek tragedy and Roman history, contribute to the rebirth of tragic literature?

At this point, the only conclusion that may be drawn from Petrarch's discussion of this subject in his da Carrara letter is that he considers power to be mysterious. The ways in which it is acquired, preserved, and finally lost cannot easily be explained, as they often have little to do with social and political conditions; rather, they involve the personal and psychological dynamics at work among the small ruling elite. This fact, however, should not compel us to dismiss Petrarch's study of politics as totally naive or void of historical interest. Petrarch is not just a scholar and a poet who briefly touches on matters outside of his intellectual domain. On the contrary, in his psychological analysis of power, he shows all of his modernity.

Over a century after Petrarch, Machiavelli, unknowingly concluding the age of Renaissance Humanism, said in *The Prince* that often the only way a ruler can keep his power is through repression and other cruel means. Machiavelli sadly concluded that these are the only means through which the ruler can keep human passions under control and prevent well-known tragedies, both personal and political, such as tyrannicide. Machiavelli actually expressed the extreme consequence of a line of thought that already appeared quite evident in Petrarch's writings. In the same passage where he established that a prince can keep his power only through love, Petrarch almost

contradicts himself by offering an ambivalent analysis of what love
is or could be:

> Who can have such a hard heart not to reciprocate an honest
> love? A dishonest love, in fact, is not love, but hatred disguised
> under an honest name and should be reciprocated not with love
> but with hatred. And, in fact, what is it to reciprocate the love
> of him who loves you in an evil way if not to promote a crime
> through a crime and to become an accomplice to the criminality
> of others. Without dwelling on that let us therefore return to
> honest love.[12]

Petrarch continues by saying that Augustus is an example of the
honest "father of the state" while Nero represents a dishonest one.
But where is the line to be drawn separating the honest from the
dishonest? Who is the expert of human psychology capable of consis-
tently discerning the real motivations of a prince's actions? Petrarch
has no answer. But what he does say is complex and far-reaching for
Renaissance culture and the history of the Brutus figure. The human
soul is a mysterious embodiment of human passions that have a
pervasive influence on all aspects of life, including politics. When
discussing and analyzing governments and principalities, historical
conditions and necessities are but a part of the elements to be considered. The psychological dynamics of the ruling elite—the personal
loves and enmities, the envy and jealousy—also play a major part in
shaping political events. Thus Petrarch sets the groundwork for
future development, both in political treatises and in literature, of
the study of the dynamics of power based on the study of human
psychology.

A confirmation of Petrarch's highly moral point of view appears
rather surprisingly in Boccaccio, an author best known today for his
collection of often sexually overt stories *The Decameron*. In another
work, *De casibus virorum illustrium* (*The Fate of Famous Men*), written
around 1360, Boccaccio looks at human events and actions as they
relate to eternity. Adopting a Dantesque and quasi-mystical stance,
he does not judge historical events and individual deeds according to
their actual worth when they occurred; he evaluates them as they
appear to him long after those who carried them out have died. On
the whole, the work is an indictment of human vanity that tries to
show that all the trappings of greatness and power craved by the

ambitious have no importance when evaluated against eternity. The very title of the work is indicative of this assumption: the Latin word *casus* (the nominative case of *casibus* used in Boccaccio's title) means both "fate" and "fall." The title could therefore be translated also as *The Fall of Famous Men*. The author imagines himself alone in his study when many of the greatest men and women of all time appear to him in despondent circumstances, begging to be included in his history:

> As I was trying to find out what utility, with all of my studies, I could bring to the state, a larger than expected quantity of matter offered itself; and with special poignancy, there became fixed in my mind the obscene voluptuousness of princes and others who are in power, the terrible excesses, the sinful laziness, the insatiable desires, the hatreds that stream with blood, the sudden and cruel revenges, the endless nefarious crimes.[13]

Brutus is hardly mentioned in the entire work. In fact he is only briefly identified, along with Cassius, as a parricide in a chapter featuring characters involved in the civil wars and in other events concerning Caesar.[14] Moreover, Boccaccio does not explain why he calls Brutus a parricide, which seems to indicate an uncritical use of the term, possibly an unconscious compliance with the medieval tradition and Dante's assessment of the episode. The tyrannicide motive appears elsewhere in reference to the killing of Caesar, even when Brutus and Cassius are not mentioned.[15] However, at the beginning of the work, Boccaccio, in retelling the story of Jocasta, Laius, and Oedipus as well as other stories of Greek history and mythology, understands that power and parricide are often intertwined. It is not the tragic aspect of parricide, both real and, as in the case of Brutus, allegorical, that seems to interest him in this work. Boccaccio's intention is to offer a completely moral view of power, one that follows the Christian system of ethics. He reprimands the sons of powerful men for being impatient to take over their fathers' roles too soon, no matter the cost. On the other hand, he deplores rulers for their tendency to become blinded by the power they have obtained and to believe that cruelty is the basis for the only workable form of government:

> He who governs must remember that the governed are not slaves but collaborators. Just as regal honor is enhanced by the

work of the governed, the king's care must procure peace and welfare for his people. Let God see how the princes of our times behave. The inclinations of the princes are all towards tyranny; and despising the impotence of their subjects, they want to shine with gold and gems, be surrounded by a long line of servants, build big palaces, entertain many concubines. . . .[16]

In meeting with and speaking to the great men and women of the past in their afterlives as Dante did, Boccaccio learns that the material privileges for which they strove while living on earth were pure illusions. Boccaccio obviously accepts power as a necessity of civil living and calls those who killed Caesar parricides. His treatise is not intended, as some later Humanist works will be, as a criticism of power. He does however repeat again and again that power brings with it a blindness that can turn anyone into a cruel and unreasonably greedy tyrant. Boccaccio does not even suggest how this can be avoided; he simply calls for the king's self-restraint. All including the king, Boccaccio says, should fear the coming of a universal judgment that will display a power far greater than the enjoyment of all the material goods a king can amass. The consequences of the final judgment are eternal, while the privileges of power and wealth are too soon taken away—if not by misfortune, then certainly by death:

And therefore why, oh we unfortunate, do we, blinded with such passion, aspire to higher things? Why do we become so lofty when we reach them? Why do we rely on mortal things even if we know that a small mist can cover and obfuscate the great light? We must therefore repress, admonished by the example of those who came before us, this insatiable desire and with unbending virtue we must keep it under control, so that, content with very little, we may humbly deserve to attain the real glory.[17]

Boccaccio's argument, the moral argument opposing the glory of power and of material goods to the glory coming from a universal and metahistorical view of human events, will not be the prevailing one in the centuries that followed. Beginning with the fifteenth century, in what appears to be a preparation for Machiavelli's famous separation of morality from any issue involving political power, the question of government will be a question in itself. In writings on power's many facets, morality will be the least important. By and large the discussion, no matter how many historical examples and metaphors it may use, will focus primarily on the acquisition and maintenance of power.

This is not terribly surprising if one considers that during the fifteenth century various European countries tried to reinforce their identity as states and to create, whenever possible, a centralized bureaucracy. The state became a primary concern. In the language of politics a new term was soon to be created in order to justify any action, no matter how morally deplorable, if committed in the name of the state: *ragion di stato* in Italian, *raison d'état* in French, and "reason of state" in English. This term and the state of mind that accompanies it will stream with blood for over five hundred years and will contain within its own perverse logic the reason for its own justification. It will also be the principle by which modern Western states will be able to develop, prosper, and dominate. The issue of morality will not surface again with as much importance, as found in Dante and in general in most authors up to the fourteenth century, until the twentieth century, when the actions of Hitler and Stalin, as well as many more recent events, prove that the religion of politics can be carried out to the extremes of fanaticism and folly.[18]

Fifteenth-Century Florentine Debates on Tyranny

The debate on power with its many references to Roman history and especially to the assassination of Caesar reached in the treatises of the early fifteenth century an unprecedented richness of intellectual fervor and interest. The best political minds were interested in the relationship between those who held power and those who were governed. In addition, because of the Renaissance's infatuation with the history of Rome and its leaders, classical events inevitably became the yardstick against which current events and political problems were evaluated. With power as the predominant subject, the relationship between Brutus and Caesar became the official metaphor for the study of the relationship between limited, or republican, power and absolute power.

Was Caesar really a tyrant or was he simply trying to modernize the Roman institutions? What is a tyrant? Is tyranny the necessary form of government in times of instability? Is tyranny necessarily always an evil? How is the state preserved from the danger of tyranny? How can the people prevent their rulers from becoming tyrants? Are not tyrannical methods sometimes the only recourse available to the leader in order to suppress internal discord and preserve the integrity of the state? These questions and many more agitated the minds of Italian politicians at the beginning of the fifteenth century and created a political debate unique for its intensity and wealth of new ideas. For a few years between the end of the fourteenth century and the beginning of the fifteenth, the political debate encompassed all aspects of the humanities. A combination of history and rhetoric used in the discussion of matters relating to the Republic allowed for meditations on all areas of philosophy. The Humanists were convinced that the proper understanding of the institution of government would entail an understanding of human nature as a whole. In fact, in this principle lies the secret of Humanism: the assumption that all aspects of human activity are interconnected and that political institutions and forms of government should be considered not only on the basis of which one would ideally be the best, but also according to a more universal view of human events. The concepts of fortune, fate, and predestination acquire a crucial importance in this context.

The individual, it is true, was viewed as being in control of personal destiny. To deny this would be equivalent to denying one of the founding principles of Renaissance philosophy. However, humankind's liberty to shape the individual's future cannot escape the judgment of superior forces, symbolized at times as destiny, and at times more directly as God. In creating a vision of human action that tries to account both for human freedom and for the role of destiny, Renaissance philosophy created a puzzle that would eventually lead to a tragic vision of human affairs. The medieval point of view, the most liberal side of which Dante expressed rather faithfully, forced human freedom to comply with God's will. In a famous similitude Dante states that freedom is not limited by the fact that human actions are known in advance by God, just as a ship going down a river is free to veer where it pleases, although someone who watches it from a distance knows in advance, like God, what path it will follow.[19] It was Dante's intention to establish an harmony between God's will and human action.

In the Renaissance, while the ideas about destiny remained basically the same, the emphasis was placed on the differences between human desires and historical necessity. Although the individual was still seen as subjected to destiny by the inability to oppose fate, this view was considered a limitation that contrasted with the Renaissance idea of freedom of the will. The inability to oppose destiny constitutes humankind's weakness, its tragic flaw. In celebrating the greatness of humankind the Renaissance expressed the hope that the individual would ultimately be able to keep destiny in check. This was Machiavelli's dream in *The Prince*.

The Humanists' agreement with Dante on the issue of Brutus was actually only superficial. They considered his act against Caesar not a sin but a tragic failure against superior forces such as destiny and God, forces much larger than Brutus' human dimension. Assessments of Brutus' act that agree with Dante always carried with them the tragic feeling that it would have been better if historical conditions had been more favorable to Brutus' views and ideals. Because of this basic cultural difference, the consideration of Brutus as a parricide, so dear to Dante, appears only metaphorically in Renaissance political treatises. The attempt to oppose destiny may be considered a tragic failure but never an act of parricide. The theme of the parricide will be proposed again only in tragedy, partially in homage to classical tragic models and partially because in the highly metaphorical language of High Renaissance theatre the identification of *destiny* with *father* produces a richness of meanings that is appealing from a literary point of view. After all, no matter how evolved, articulate, and sophisticated the discussion on the Republic becomes, old ideas always seem to reappear in one form or another. And the idea identifying *destiny* with *father*, together representing the path devised for our lives by supernatural and biological forces, is one of the oldest, probably preceding classical and literate cultures altogether and originating in the primitive worship rituals of tribal societies where divinities and the elders of the group are coupled together as symbols of destiny.

It should not be surprising, therefore, that the Florentine Coluccio Salutati, who at the beginning of the fifteenth century initiated the lively debate on the assassination of Caesar with his famous *De Tyranno (On Tyranny)*, wrote an earlier work entitled *De fato et fortuna (On Fate and Fortune)*, a complex and thought-provoking analysis of the relation between free will and destiny. Born in 1331 in a small Tuscan town, Salutati considered himself a citizen of Florence, the city where he served as secretary from 1375 to his death in 1406. A Humanist and a scholar, he cultivated Latin literature and rediscovered many forgotten classical works. He corresponded regularly with Petrarch and Boccaccio, and from Petrarch he developed his love for classical rhetoric and Cicero. A republican and a lover of liberty, Salutati saw a parallel between the greatness of his own Florentine republic and that of Rome. The search for analogies likening the two cities was a constant intellectual occupation for Salutati's Humanist predisposition. However, his meditations on Roman history with an emphasis on the period of the transition from the Republic to the Empire illustrate the complexity and depth of his intellect and philosophy. His own republican ideals clashed with Dante's defense of the Empire and in general with the medieval and Augustinian tradition largely based on Seneca, a philosopher Salutati nevertheless greatly admired. How was he going to find a compromise between freedom, the republican freedom he so strongly believed in that is represented in Roman history by the figure of Brutus, and the wisdom of history, a metaphor for the will of God and destiny? Was it not God's will to bring about the establishment of the Empire? But did Salutati really need a compromise between such opposing concepts?

In the *De Tyranno,* as we shall see, Salutati tries to settle the dispute between Caesar and Brutus without having to glorify one and condemn the other the way Dante did. But in order to achieve this goal he first had to come to terms with the nature of history and of destiny. He had, in other words, to discuss the role of individual responsibility and clarify in his own mind how guilty one makes oneself when one decides to commit acts that are, without one knowing it, contrary to the will of God. This search is carried out in the long and complex *De fato et fortuna,* a philosophical treatise divided into three parts, written between 1396 and 1397. In this work Salutati finds the same philosophical contrast between free will and destiny that he saw in history between Brutus and Caesar. By viewing the problem from this point of view Salutati, who reaches the same conclusion as Dante, is able to articulate his understanding of the Brutus-Caesar episode quite differently from that of the poet. In Dante, Brutus—a name that for Salutati combines the historical Brutus and the Brutus symbolizing parricide—is treated as a sinner for having tried to oppose God's will regarding the coming of the Roman Empire. To the Humanists, Dante's punishment of Brutus appears as a limitation of free will because Dante assumes that the universal will of God was evident to Brutus and therefore should have prevented his act. But from a Renaissance point of view, the assumption that the coming of the Empire was willed by destiny should not have limited Brutus' freedom to act according to his beliefs. In those chapters of the *De fato et fortuna* in which freedom of the will is discussed, Salutati brings up the question of destiny in relation to Caesar's assassination:

Many say: "Divine providence is infallible." I believe that this is true and also in accordance with religion, and it would be not only sacrilegious, but also very stupid to deny it. "Divine providence is therefore infallible; what God has seen in advance will happen without fail." And this must be believed without contention. Then, more: "What will happen without failure, what cannot be in any other way, has to happen necessarily." And this too, if you understand it well, cannot be denied. "Therefore, since God from eternity saw in advance that Brutus would kill Caesar in the Senate and that this would happen without fail and could not be any other way, it follows that Brutus would necessarily kill Caesar." And this is easy to answer. Since, in fact, we assume that "God from eternity saw in advance that Brutus would kill Caesar," we do not assume the same thing, as it is proper, about the providence of the supreme being. Because God saw in advance not simply that Brutus would kill the dictator, but that he would kill him not necessarily but according to contingency and through his free will.[20]

The complexity of Salutati's argument, which borders on sophistry and expresses a rhetorical and legalistic frame of mind, should not deter us from understanding the philosophical importance of his thinking. Unlike Dante, Salutati does not want the coming of the Empire as willed by God to cause an automatic condemnation of Brutus. In preparing the basis for an evaluation of Brutus in accordance with Renaissance principles, Salutati asserts the dignity of freedom of choice yet does not want to compromise his own republican beliefs by criticizing those of Brutus. However, he had to consider that history chose to have Caesar's political program succeed and Brutus' fail. Salutati realized that, despite Caesar's assassination, the Roman Republic had exhausted its role and the city was ready for a new order.

Salutati concluded that Brutus was guilty of nothing else but being human. He fought for his own ideals to the very end, not aware, as humans never are, that higher forces were guiding the course of history in a direction opposite to the one he favored. He may be a fallen hero, as well as a tragic hero, but never a guilty one.

Salutati's analysis of the Brutus character in *De fato et fortuna* does not take into account Dante's position, except for an affirmation of Dante's belief in free will as expressed in the sixteenth canto of the *Purgatory*. But Dante, the great poet and the glory of the Florentines, could not be overlooked, as difficult and embarrassing as it may have been to squarely face his accusation and unequivocal punishment of Brutus in the *Inferno*. Dante uses little sophistry regarding Brutus' sin; Brutus is equaled only by Judas in terms of who was given the worst punishment in *The Divine Comedy*.

Salutati deals with Dante's accusation of Brutus in his later work, *De Tyranno* (*On Tyranny*) written in 1400. The *De Tyranno* is a defense of Dante disguised as a treatise on tyranny written in a strictly rhetorical, deductive, and legalistic way. It is divided into five chapters, each establishing a point that is further developed in the following chapter. The thrust of the treatise becomes very clear just by listing the chapter titles: "What is the meaning of 'tyrant' and what is the origin of the name," "Whether it is good to kill the tyrant," "On Caesar's reign and whether he reasonably can or must be listed among the tyrants," "Whether Julius Caesar was justifiably killed," and "Why Dante rightfully placed Brutus and Cassius in lower hell as the worst traitors."

In the first two chapters, after having established that the tyrant is the one who illegally acquires and then abuses power, Salutati states quite simply that the tyrant should be killed. His argument becomes if not totally convoluted at least somewhat complicated in the third chapter, where, in order to prove at a later point that Caesar was unjustly assassinated, Salutati must first prove that he was not a tyrant.

The defense of Caesar by the secretary of the Florentine Republic is in all respects a masterpiece of Renaissance rhetoric. Salutati hardly discusses the facts of Caesar's life and political career and uses Petrarch, who had criticized Cicero's ambiguous position on Caesar, as the starting point of his argument. In progressing a step beyond Petrarch, Salutati quotes from Cicero a series of statements that are clearly favorable to Caesar in order to prove Cicero's opportunism, which made him a pro-Caesarean while Caesar was alive and an anti-Caesarean after Caesar was dead. Salutati supports his argument by saying that Caesar brought peace among opposing factions and that "according to law and without injury maintained the reign in the common republic."[21] The ambiguity of this last statement, which closes the third chapter, should sufficiently indicate the intellectual acrobatics Salutati undertakes to save the glory of the Florentine poet while not completely betraying the republican ideal. Only by having a blind faith in the power of rhetoric can one not find a contradiction between "the reign," which Salutati claims Caesar was holding over

Rome, and the "common republic" on which the reign was exercised. Interestingly, the defense of Caesar conducted in this chapter with so few references to the historical events of Caesar's life is largely based on a criticism of Cicero's writings. Rhetoric, the Ciceronian rhetoric that Petrarch had at once admired and found so ambiguous, was for Salutati taking the place of historical analysis; to prove a historical point it was sufficient to find the proper compromise between opposing words and the ideas they represent. Finally, the possibility that this criticism of Cicero actually disguises an admiration for him should not be overlooked. In using Cicero rather than history as his point of departure for his analysis, Salutati is also setting himself up for a competition with the champion of the art he is using. He is actually trying to beat Cicero at his own game, to be a better rhetorician than he was.

The fourth chapter of the *De Tyranno* uses all the ammunition gained in the previous section to prove the injustice committed against Caesar by Brutus, Cassius, and the other conspirators. Again the thrust of the argument is highly rhetorical and Ciceronian, more like a learned dispute than an analysis of political and historical events, and again the villain is Cicero, caught changing his mind about Caesar after Caesar was dead: "I am surprised to see my Cicero so full of anger toward the memory of the dictator, that he not only said that he was rightfully killed, but also considered justifiable all those who pushed for his death with incitations, or willed it with their votes, or approved of it with their statements."[22] Salutati indignantly argues that Caesar's killing was beyond question an act of treason. Most of the conspirators had, in fact, received Caesar's favors and enjoyed his protection and friendship: "And who can believe that they were all good, those who were affected by Caesar's generosity, and some had their lives saved by him, and others received all the trappings of high status, and who, all of a sudden, became so ungrateful that they all willed and approved of his death?"[23]

This argument, along with another anti-Ciceronian tirade assessing Caesar's role as a great pacifier of the civil discords among the various Roman factions, leads Salutati to conclude the fourth chapter with a vindication of Caesar as a ruler: "For these reasons we conclude that those killers of Caesar did not kill the tyrant, but killed the father of the land and the most merciful and legitimate ruler of the world, and that they grievously erred against the republic, as grievious and hateful as it can be to incite the furor and the madness of civil war in a peaceful republic."[24]

The fifth and final chapter constitutes Salutati's ultimate agreement with Dante on the punishment of Brutus and Cassius. To make his case even stronger, he dwells on the tradition of Brutus as a parricide. This legend derived in part from Brutus' mother, Servilia, and Caesar being lovers and in part from Suetonius' report that as Brutus was raising his dagger against Caesar, Caesar said: "*Kai su teknon*" ("And you too, my son").[25] Salutati probably knew that Caesar was Brutus' father only symbolically, although a highly forceful symbol. He did not use the parricide theme in the *De fato et fortuna*, probably so as not to undermine the strictly philosophical nature of the work. But he felt free to use it in the *De Tyranno* precisely because of the different nature and genre of this work, aimed at displaying all of his virtuosity as a rhetorician.

The philosophical implications of the *De Tyranno*, compared with those of the *De fato et fortuna*, evidence a complete about-face. In the earlier work Salutati affirmed that Brutus' act was conducted in a state of total free will, although it might have contrasted with the course of history as willed by God. According to Christian morality, an act committed in a state of total free will is never a sinful act since it expresses the individual's highest level of consciousness. Indeed, Salutati's affirmation of Brutus' free will in the killing of Caesar also expresses the author's Humanist and republican feelings, aimed at stressing the importance of individual freedom and dignity. Finally, it emphasizes the importance of the participation of the individual in the affairs of the state, forcefully pointing out that everyone has a stake in shaping the Republic's future. The only possible way to explain such a radical change of view in the *De Tyranno*, a work composed only three years after the *De fato et fortuna*, is to assume that in writing the *De Tyranno* Salutati had a different intention in mind than that of composing a philosophical treatise on the nature of destiny and of free will. In the *De Tyranno* Salutati takes issue directly with Cicero, the undisputed master of rhetoric, and challenges him to a rhetorical duel on the question of whether Caesar was a tyrant or not.

The *De Tyranno* also has the characteristics of a *querelle* (quarrel) between the ancients and the moderns, with Salutati striving to prove that he, as a modern, can outsmart Cicero, his great predecessor. The contradiction between the two different works of the same author is obviously still there but in this new light looks like a contradiction between a philosophical and a literary genre rather than a contradiction within the mind of the same man. Rhetoric and eloquence are

both akin to sophistry, as all three aim at convincing.[26] To take a
position in a rhetorical treatise therefore does not necessarily mean
that that position is believed to be true; it simply means that it can
be upheld with some degree of rationality. By taking one point of
view in the *De fato et fortuna* and the opposite in the *De Tyranno*—the
latter also being a point of view that clearly contradicts his republican
ideas—Salutati is setting the basis for a metaphorical usage of language. He is demonstrating that words have many levels of meaning
and that history can be constantly rewritten by those who can use
language creatively. Salutati, in the end, is upholding rhetorical language as one of the most effective instruments of politics, as it is
instrumental in the art of persuasion.

All aspects of Salutati's writings on Brutus and Caesar reappear,
with a greater degree of sophistication and with a larger awareness of
complexity, in the writings of one of Salutati's pupil, the Florentine
Leonardo Bruni. A Humanist well versed in Greek and Latin, Leonardo Bruni started his political career at the papal court of Innocent
VII. In 1415 he settled permanently in Florence and was secretary
of the Republic from 1427 until his death in 1444. As such he shared
many of his teacher's ideals, including his love of freedom and the
Republic and his belief in the educational and exemplary value of the
classics.

Coluccio Salutati's *De Tyranno* is a dispute between the author
and Cicero; in the *Ad Petrum Paulum Histrum Dialogus (A Dialogue
Dedicated to Pier Paolo Vergerio)*, Leonardo Bruni substantially develops Salutati's genre and themes. The dialogue, actually a composition
of two dialogues probably written between 1401 and 1405, is a *querelle
des anciens et des modernes*, maybe the first of the many *querelles*
between the old and the new culture that have appeared from the
Renaissance to the present.[27] The dialogue is also an interesting
example of the new genre of philosophical modernism, as it evaluates
how the Italian "modern" writers Dante, Petrarch, and Boccaccio
stand in comparison with the classics. Inevitably, though, the discussion involves Dante's judgment in his treatment of Brutus. Not
surprisingly, Coluccio Salutati, who had expressed his own modernism in the *De Tyranno* when showing Cicero's failures, becomes one
of the major characters of the Bruni work. The first part of the
dialogue, in which the participants are the author himself, Coluccio
Salutati, the Humanist and collector of classical manuscripts Niccolo'
Niccoli, and another minor Humanist, Roberto Rossi, is a dispute
on the art of the dialogue. In it Niccoli functions as the detractor of

modern times, claiming that the lack of books and of learning from which Florence is suffering makes it impossible for the scholars of his age to equal the greatness of the classicists, especially Cicero. Niccoli offers his panegyric in honor of Cicero, and, by comparing the moderns to Cicero, he claims the superiority of ancient learning over modern learning. The dialogue, which is modeled by Bruni after Cicero's own *De Oratore*, continues with Salutati's rebuttal of Niccoli's thesis. A tongue-in-cheek tone is not difficult to perceive in the structure of this work. In a Ciceronian dialogue, Niccoli is portrayed as he extols the glory of his master in the presence of Salutati, author of the treatise, *De Tyranno*, which is very critical of Cicero. Moreover, since the topic of the discussion is the quality of modern rhetoric versus ancient rhetoric, Bruni's dialogue appears almost as a work within a work, a rhetorical dialogue in which the disputants argue the quality of the art of the dialogue. This highly rhetorical structure reaches its apex when, following Salutati's exaltation of Dante, Petrarch, and Boccaccio as the three modern authors who do not fear a comparison with the ancients, Niccoli attacks Dante for his treatment of Brutus:

> It is much more serious and much more intolerable that he [Dante] inflicted supreme condemnation on Marcus Brutus, a man distinguished for his justice, modesty, greatness of soul, and finally for every other virtue; and this because he killed Caesar, reclaiming freedom for the Roman people, taking it from the robber's jaws. By contrast he places Junius Brutus in the Elysian Fields for the killing of the kings. But Tarquin received his kingdom from his elders and had been made a king according to law. Caesar instead usurped power with the strength of arms, and, after killing the best citizens, abolished the freedom of his country. Therefore, if Marcus Brutus was evil, Junius must be considered a lot more evil; and if on the contrary one must praise Junius for killing the king, why not extol to the sky Marcus who eliminated a tyrant? And I pass over, by Jupiter, what I am ashamed to admit was written by a Christian: that almost the same punishment can be inflicted on the man who betrayed a tyrant and on the man who sold the Savior of the world.[28]

The comparison between Marcus Brutus and the mythical Lucius Junius Brutus, leader of the movement to free Rome from the rule of Tarquin the Proud and killer of his own sons for plotting a monarchical restoration, complicates the Brutus issue further. This ancient comparison dates back at least to the times of Plutarch, who reported that Marcus Brutus was believed to be a descendant of Lucius Junius Brutus.[29] As always with Roman genealogy, descent in old, aristocratic families carries with it a host of inherited political roles and duties. In this case, the Brutuses appeared coupled in the legend and in genealogy by their love of freedom. Why would Dante, Niccoli seems to imply in his question, modify the traditional view of the Brutuses by placing the initiator of their genealogy in the Elysian Fields and punishing Marcus in the lowest pit of hell? That by doing so Dante may also indirectly criticize the classical concept of inherited social and political roles in favor of individual choice occurs neither to Niccoli nor to Coluccio Salutati when he again attempts his defense of Dante, now made more difficult by the previous accusations. Thus, a problem with a rather easy solution from a philosophical point of view becomes rather puzzling when seen exclusively through the eyes of the rhetorician. In order to solve these difficulties, Leonardo Bruni, the author of the dialogue, resorts to a solution teeming with artistry, one that parades all of rhetoric's complexity and potentiality.

In the continuation of the dialogue the following day in a different setting and with the addition of one participant, Pier di ser Mini, Salutati, when asked to make his defense of Dante, Petrarch, and Boccaccio, declines and says that Leonardo Bruni can make a comparable defense. Leonardo Bruni, while also declining to defend the authors, does offer to be the moderator in the battle between the ancients and the moderns. He then orders Niccoli to take the viewpoint contrary to the one he took the day before by defending Dante, Petrarch, and Boccaccio. For his part, Salutati is to listen and to attack Niccoli's arguments. The roles of Salutati and Niccoli are thus reversed, a solution that Salutati applauds by saying that there is "no better medicine than the one that heals a sickness with its contrary."[30]

Niccoli surprises his audience and Bruni surprises his readers with the former's response. Niccoli begins his counterpoint by retracting his statements of the previous day. He explains that his criticism of Dante, Petrarch, and Boccaccio only functioned to excite Salutati's eloquence and to force him to speak highly of the three great writers. The retraction does not, however, satisfy the group, and Niccoli is forced to defend the authors with his own arguments. Niccoli initially praises Dante's imagination and linguistic elegance and then refutes those points on which the day before he had based his criticism of the poet. The most important question regarding Brutus is treated by Niccoli in an original way that allows him to defend Dante while not really renouncing his own ideas:

> As for the third accusation, that he [Dante] attributed the same punishment to the man who killed the Savior and to the man who killed the destructor of the world, we find ourselves before the same misunderstanding that we saw during the age of Cato;[31] it is a misunderstanding that frequently deceives those fools who take the poet's expressions in a literal sense and not in a figurative one. Or do you believe that Dante, the most learned man of his times, did not know how Caesar had seized power? And that Dante did not know that Caesar had suffocated freedom? That with great pain for the Roman people the crown had been placed by Marcus Anthony on Caesar's head? Can you believe that Dante did not know how much virtue all histories attribute to Brutus? Who is it who does not praise justice, integrity, alacrity and greatness of soul? Dante did not ignore all of these things but wanted to represent in Caesar the legitimate prince, the very just ruler of the world, and in Brutus the seditious, turbulent, and evil man, who wickedly killed the prince. Brutus was not really that; how could the Senate in fact praise him for restoring liberty? But since Caesar reigned, and because Brutus, along with over sixty of the most noble citizens, killed him, the poet derived from this material for his fictions. How, otherwise, could he place a very good and just man, restorer of liberty, in the jaws of Lucifer? Why does Virgil, after all, imagine a very pure woman, who died in order to preserve her purity, as a woman completely out of control who killed herself for love? Painters and poets were always allowed to fantasize a little. Maybe, on the other hand, the thesis that Brutus committed an evil deed by killing Caesar has some substance. There are authors in fact who claim, either for partisan reasons or to pay homage to the emperors, that Brutus's act was evil and wicked. However, in order to defend that sort of parallelism between Christ and Caesar the first argument seems more convincing; and I have no doubt that this is what the poet believed.[32]

Niccoli is not simply using his rhetorical skill to prove that he can say, within the same speech, both one thing and its opposite. He and

Leonardo Bruni are probably unknowingly pushing rhetoric to where it also reveals itself as an art of interpretation. Niccoli points out such a view of rhetoric when he says that literature should be read figuratively and allegorically as well as literally and historically. Any text, Niccoli says, contains many levels of meaning. In Dante's treatment of the Brutus episode, Brutus and Caesar are not taken literally and historically but symbolically, with Brutus representing the evil plotter and Caesar the just king. That Dante believed, historically and literally, that Brutus was evil and that Caesar was just is illogical. In fact, Niccoli adds, Dante quite possibly believed the exact opposite. In closing, Niccoli also offers another argument in favor of Dante; he claims that according to some classical writers one could say that Brutus was actually evil and Caesar just but concludes that the first argument is a stronger one.

Rhetorically Leonardo Bruni's *Dialogus* represents the exact opposite of Coluccio Salutati's *De Tyranno*. In the *De Tyranno* Salutati's defense of Dante is historical as he intends to show that Caesar was indeed a good leader and that Cicero's attitudes towards him were based on opportunism. Bruni's angle is much more complex and sophisticated. Before dealing with the facts related by the literature under consideration, Bruni discusses the nature of literature itself. He believes that to understand literature, to deem it reasonable, we do not need to manipulate the facts of history so that they coincide with our ideas. On the contrary, we must be able to distinguish between historical facts and the allegories and the myths that are created by historical facts, especially when they are particularly eventful. The facts surrounding the life and death of Caesar have acquired through time such an overwhelming symbolic value that no specific person can be held responsible for their distortion. The symbolic personas of Brutus and Caesar have become both separated from and confused with the historical ones. Such duplicity, creating an interplay between fact and fiction, is one of the major legacies of the Renaissance to modern times.

At the same time Bruni's work contains an almost heroic attempt at interpretation that anticipates the attitude of critics of the Enlightenment who aimed at a total revision of Western literary history to clearly separate truth from falsehood. In its codifying mania, the Enlightenment created various categories of textuality and attributed to each a precise function in the realm of knowledge. Similarly, in his defense of Dante on the second day, Niccolo' Niccoli anticipates this attitude as he clearly establishes the difference between poetry

as the realm of fantasy and prose, in the style of history, as the realm
of truth. After the poetical, and therefore fictional, nature of Dante's
work has been established, the poet no longer needs to be considered
a falsifier and a distorter of reality.

Obviously, this sort of critical approach immensely complicates
the discussion on textuality that started at the beginning of the Renaissance. Literary works are not easy to classify in genres. Often, fiction
and history are intermingled in a literary text, making it difficult to
distinguish between truth and falsehood. Bruni's almost mathemati-
cal formula identifying poetry with falsehood and prose with truth
stands at the beginning of the modern history of exegesis, a history
which through the centuries will produce many different philosophies
of textuality.

Leonardo Bruni's allegorical interpretation of the Brutus episode
possibly found an almost immediate echo in one of the greatest works
of literary criticism of the fifteenth century, Cristoforo Landino's
famous *Commento sopra la Commedia (Commentary on the Divine Comedy)* of 1481, which was subsequently published with Botticelli's
illustrations. The book reproduces *The Divine Comedy* with intertex-
tual comments by Landino on large folio pages, resembling an ex-
tended annotated edition of modern times. The lengthy commentary
on Brutus is almost a short essay. In extensive reflections on the
central part of canto 34 of the *Inferno,* which regards Brutus and
Cassius, Landino sums up the entire quattrocento discussion on the
subject, from both a political and a literary point of view. After saying
that Dante praises Caesar not for being a just man but as the symbol
of the Emperor, Landino writes:

> And Brutus and Cassius, who killed him [Caesar], he [Dante]
> does not place them [in hell] as Brutus and Cassius but as
> those who killed the true monarch. Similarly he places Cato in
> purgatory, who according to our faith could in no way be saved,
> not as the soul of Cato, but as [a symbol for] the liberty which
> he strongly defended. And it would have certainly been an
> unbelievable cruelty, and one totally alien to the doctrine and
> justice of this poet, to inflict for eternity such a strong punish-
> ment on those who, for a burning passion, confronted death to
> free the state from the yoke of servitude. Had they been Christi-
> ans such action would have given them a place in the highest
> heaven. I do not deny that Caesar was endowed with many
> different and excellent virtues. But as soon as such terrible

impiety was born in him and, hoping to become a tyrant, he crossed the river Rubicon, he changed, from an excellent man into a terrible beast. And with this sole crime he submerged and extinguished all the good things that Rome owed him. Therefore Brutus and Cassius did not kill that Caesar who, through a struggle that lasted ten years and with great difficulties and immense danger, gave the Roman people all of Gaul, all of Germany, and Britain which we call England. They [Brutus and Cassius] did not kill that Caesar who in ten years and in many battles killed with his victorious armies one million one hundred and ninety-two thousand enemies for the Roman cause. They did not kill that Caesar who was endowed with great generosity, unheard-of clemency, honored eloquence and abundant and varied knowledge. But it was he who ungratefully turned against his country the forces that he had received from it. It was he who nefariously took away the freedom from the country he was supposed to defend. And without doubt what greater virtue can there be than that of vindicating the injuries suffered by the motherland, for which every good citizen must look beyond his possessions, his children and his own life.[33]

In his comment on Dante's treatment of the Brutus episode Landino brings to fruition the critical system cleverly devised by Bruni. Landino's language presents the difference between the historical and symbolic figures as a matter of course: "And Brutus and Cassius, . . . [Dante] does not place them [in hell] as Brutus and Cassius, but as those who killed the true monarch." By Landino's time the difference between history and myth was no longer a cause for controversy.

Widely accepted in textual studies and used to discover the true meaning of classical literature, the distinction between myth and history favors the use and the abuse of history in politics. In an age that increasingly projected toward the future—a modernism crucially expressed by Salutati's defense of the modern poets in Bruni's dialogue—intellectuals were quickly freeing themselves from the myths of the past. Brutus was bound to become, more and more so, the liberator. Poetically he may have remained the villain, but politically he was becoming a fashionable historical model.

The Brutus Fashion

By the time in which Landino was writing his commentary on *The Divine Comedy*, Brutus was no longer only a literary character. The influence of and fascination with classical culture and history was so pervasive and extensive that its heroes spilled over from the treatises and the meditations of scholarly writers and became again living actors. For about sixty years the Renaissance centers of Italy, most notably Florence, were again populated by Romans, new Romans, trying to repeat and perfect the examples of their ancient predecessors.

In the first major study of the Renaissance, *The Civilization of the Renaissance in Italy* written in 1860, Jacob Burckhardt proposes an interpretation of the period that has been overlooked or forgotten by his many followers in the revival of Renaissance studies. Burckhardt describes the fifteenth century's imitation of classical times through a comparison to modern fashion, a kind of collective mania. Classical Rome became a model not only in scholarship and in politics, but also in daily attitudes and in lifestyles. The men of the Renaissance adopted dress fashions, immortalized in paintings, reminiscent of Roman dress, the women revived cosmetic techniques forgotten since the days of Cleopatra and Messalina, and parents gave Latin and Greek names to their children. "The nation was, and is, vain;" writes Burckhardt about Italy, "and even serious men among it looked on a handsome and becoming costume as an element in the perfection of the individual."[34]

We have, by now, become accustomed to considering fashion as a typically twentieth-century phenomenon, one that possibly became popular at the turn of the century in Paris. Such words as *mode*, *vogue*, and *à la page* in French and *moda* and *voga* in Italian (along with their antonyms *passé* and *passato*) convey an inherently contemporary flavor. They indicate our modern need to change constantly, even in appearance, to something different and, especially, to something that is better than what we had before. To be a la mode is the contrary of being classic, a term derived from historical language and used to describe a lifestyle that indicates permanence rather than mutability. Because fashion is often associated with superficiality, we automatically refuse to apply it to the Renaissance, a period of the past we often tend to revere. However, reflection may remind us that during the Renaissance fashion revealed itself for the first time as a fairly widespread phenomenon.

How can we explain, if not through fashion, the Renaissance infatuation with the Romans and, at the same time, the equally strongly held idea, so clearly expressed by Coluccio Salutati in Bruni's *Dialogus,* of the Renaissance as a modern cultural phenomenon? Does not fashion express the need to identify with a certain external image while maintaining the awareness that the image does not really represent the reality? In their attempt to be Romans, the people of the Renaissance were conscious that they were moderns imitating the ancients and the classics. They were doing something fashionable, something à la mode, and *di moda*. After all, the concepts of "modern" and "fashionable" are culturally associated. In the Romance languages both *moderne* or *moderno* and *mode* or *moda* are derived from the same Latin adverb *modo* (recent, of the last minute).[35]

Although Renaissance classicism has been identified at least in part as a fashion, its effect, both cultural and historical, has in no way been diminished. Probably more powerful than culture itself, fashion penetrates the tempers of those most susceptible to its influence, namely the ambitious and the narcissistic who look out to the external world to find admiration and roles to follow. Politics is often their favorite arena, and the Renaissance's Roman fashion plays itself out at its best in the realm of politics. As Burckhardt writes:

> As to the imitation of antiquity, the influence of which on moral, and more especially on political, questions we shall often refer to, the example was set by the rulers themselves, who, both in their conception of the state and in their personal conduct, took the old Roman empire avowedly as their model. In like manner their opponents, when they set to work with a deliberate theory, took pattern by the ancient tyrannicides. It may be hard to prove that in the main point—in forming the resolve itself—they consciously followed a classical example; but the appeal to antiquity is no mere phrase.[36]

The tyrannicide modeled on Brutus became popular during the Renaissance. To recall some of its imitators, in just the year 1476 there were three: Gerolamo Gentile to free the city of Genova from the Milanese; Niccolo' d'Este in Ferrara against the duke Ercole; and in Milano by Lampugnani, Olgiati, and Visconti against Galeazzo Sforza. In 1478, Pope Sixtus IV, who wanted his nephew Riario to replace the Medici in ruling Florence, instigated the famous Congiura de' Pazzi (Pazzi Conspiracy) against Lorenzo de' Medici and his brother Giuliano. The Pope used members of the Pazzi family and Archbishop Salviati in his plot against the Medici. On 26 April 1478, as Lorenzo and Giuliano were attending High Mass in the cathedral, they were attacked by the conspirators. Lorenzo got away with a wound, but Giuliano was stabbed to death. The avenging Florentines captured the conspirators. The Congiura de' Pazzi inspired two great literary works; in the *Coniurationis Commentarium (Commentary on the Conspiracy)* the Humanist Angelo Poliziano, faithful to the Medici family, condemned the conspirators' act, while in the *De Libertate (On Liberty)* Alamanno Rinuccini expressed the republican and libertarian point of view.[37]

In 1513, the year of Machiavelli's *Prince,* and again in Florence, Pietro Paolo Boscoli and Agostino Capponi, the new Brutus and Cassius, attempted to carry out a plot against Giuliano, Giovanni, and Giulio de' Medici. The plot ended in failure and the conspirators were condemned to death. The night before his execution, Pietro Paolo Boscoli asked in a confession given to the Humanist historian Luca della Robbia to be pardoned for having allowed the myth of Brutus to control his actions.[38]

Finally, in the most famous and most discussed of all Renaissance conspiracies, in 1537 Lorenzino de' Medici stabbed the ruler of Florence, Duke Alessandro de' Medici, to death. After the murder Lorenzino wrote his own *Apologia (Apology)*, Michelangelo celebrated him by sculpting a bust of Brutus, and Donato Giannotti wrote a dialogue discussing the role of Brutus in Roman history.[39]

In explaining so many plots and conspiracies, many of which were made in the names of Brutus and Cassius, one must first separate politics from mythology. The conspiracies in themselves represent a reaction to a political aberration: the Italian city-state created under democratic and republican principles was quickly developing into a kind of monarchy. In most of the cities, and again the example of the Medici in Florence is here symptomatic, one leading family, usually from the rich merchant class, was gaining control of the state and abolishing in practice, if not in form, the democratic and popular system that was the base of the earlier political order. Many factors contributed to this evolution. First, the accumulation of wealth and power by one family to a degree that greatly exceeded that of other leading families created a situation of *primus inter pares* (first among equals), which is the initial step to principality. Second, the constant wars and disputes among the various Italian city-states and among different factions within each city-state indirectly created the necessity for a prince who was capable of handling emergencies and who was above the opposing parties. This evolution was a natural one that contrasted with the ideas and the ideals of many Renaissance scholars. The contradiction is no more obvious than in Machiavelli, the populist and republican secretary of the Florentine republic, who in his most famous work, *The Prince*, calls for a totalitarian ruler to restore the quickly deteriorating Italian situation. Machiavelli allows the prince to conquer and maintain power by whatever means and almost legitimizes a sort of despotic tyranny as the optimal system of government. In less than a hundred years, the quattrocento, the century that had started in the name of republican ideals, was transformed into the century of the tyrants. At its close, few cities still maintained popular and republican governments. In most, one dynasty had power firmly in its hands. This rapid transformation explains the resistance the new order encountered from those who put their ideals before necessity and who believed that their city should never succumb to despotic oppression.

Many Renaissance conspirators took Brutus, almost infallibly, as their inspirator and model for quite complex reasons. To conduct a plot against a ruler one does not need to have a model, only efficient and faithful collaborators who can act quickly and in secrecy and who do not, as so often happens, lose their courage the night before they are supposed to act. But the ascription to great classical names, and to that of Brutus in particular, as a function of good luck—a practice that was a great part of the folklore of Renaissance conspiracies— needs a different explanation. The fashion element, of course, gives an aura of distinction to anything carrying a Roman name. Also, the conspiracy that Brutus and Cassius led against Caesar, along with the ensuing political chaos, places that episode at the center of ancient history. It is certainly the most famous conspiracy of all times, and without doubt the one that historians, both ancient and modern, discussed the most. But the primary aspect of the Brutus myth that must have excited the fantasy of the Renaissance conspirators was the complexity of Brutus' personality and the difficult moral and personal development through which he reached his decision. Brutus' erudition and great interest in rhetoric and philosophy, his studies in Greece and familiarity with the best minds of his times, exonerate his act from being a purely political one and lift it to the loftier realm of the acts of the mind. In his biography of Brutus, Plutarch dwells at length on the intellectual side of Brutus' personality, showing how he was always torn between thought and action. He is described as reading books between conflicts at the battle of Pharsalus,[40] as being torn by internal psychological troubles—which also disturbed him during his sleep—resulting from Caesar's ascent to power,[41] and as being deeply in doubt as to what action to take to stop Caesar from

destroying Roman liberty. Suetonius, in his attempt to raise Caesar's
killing to tragic levels, recounts how Caesar spoke in Greek, the
language of tragedy, the famous words to Brutus, "And you too, my
son."[42]

Caesar's suspected paternity of Brutus has little historical support
but was however surmised by some of his contemporaries in view of
Brutus' mother's relationship with Caesar, adding the ingredient of
parricide to Brutus' act. As unfounded as this surmise may be, it
infuses the tragic myth of political—if not biological—parricide into
the event, signifying the idea that the king is also the "father of the
state." Finally, Brutus' ambition, his need to excel at all costs even
when the goal seems out of sight, undoubtedly inspired Renaissance
conspirators. It is best expressed in Plutarch's quotation of Caesar's
comment about Brutus: "I do not know what this young man wants,
but all that he wants he wants it very badly."[43]

If one examines the "classics of Italian conspiracies" as they started
to be called,[44] starting with the poetic infatuation of Girolamo Olgiati,
a conspirator against Duke Galeazzo Maria Sforza of Milano, a majority of them involved the inspiring ghost of Brutus. When Olgiati was
captured and then tortured after the murder, he was reported to
have talked at length about Brutus and Cassius. He wanted to be
remembered as a man in the same league as the great tyrannicides of
all times.[45]

The Florentine Conspiracies

The literary reaction to the Pazzi conspiracy was reflected in one
of the Renaissance's most interesting pieces of dramatic historical
narration and one of the best examples of the revival of classical Latin
style, Angelo Poliziano's *Coniurationis Commentarium*. The *Commentarium* is an early example of an attempt to describe a political conspiracy and to portray with some psychological depth the personalities
of the conspirators. The work draws heavily on a classical example
of this genre, Sallust's *The War with Catiline*, in which the famous
Roman historian tells the story of Catiline's conspiracy of nobles
against Caesar. Stylistically, ideologically, and structurally, Poliziano
sets himself as the new Sallust who narrates the story of a threat
brought to the state by a small group of people. Because it is, even
at a conscious level, so close to its Roman model, the *Coniurationis
Commentarium* is considered a work of imitation, written under the

great Renaissance infatuation for classical literature. Sentences and idiomatic expressions are lifted almost word for word from Sallust's text in various places, while descriptions and the entire structure of the piece closely follow the Roman example.

Poliziano's desire to appear classical by imitating Sallust is so obvious that the reader naturally questions whether the treatise was written to relate the truth about a historical event of Poliziano's times or to serve as an exercise in the imitation of the Latins. It would be fruitless to try to answer this question because the truth probably lies somewhere in between. Compelled to write about the Pazzi conspiracy, Poliziano chose Sallust as his model. He would have chosen someone else if a different topic had presented itself. But obviously Poliziano's pro-Medicean position is an authentic one, and his hatred against the conspirators coincides with Sallust's bias against Catiline and with his pro-Caesarean feelings. Something very new for the postclassical world emerged in Poliziano's description of the Pazzi conspiracy, however: the creation of the negative stereotype of the conspirator's personality. The positive stereotype was also created around this time, especially in Machiavelli's works other than *The Prince*. One way or another, the conspirator was at the center of attention.

In his description of the Pazzi conspiracy, Poliziano draws heavily on Sallust's description of Catiline and his sycophants to depict an image of the conspirators as evil and abnormal men, with lowly, almost bestial passions, who were torn by different and opposing desires. These personalities are without doubt exceptional ones; in all aspects of their lives they appear to exceed any possible classification of normality. From Poliziano's pages an image of the conspirator emerges that likens him to the modern day terrorist or the postromantic Nihilists so well described in Dostoevski. Poliziano tries to create personalities larger than life in their vices and their lifestyles in order to describe their attempt to overthrow the Medici as a monstrous one that can only be condemned. Jacopo Pazzi "gambled [with dice] all night" and was, just like Catiline in Sallust, "pale and deathly looking."[46] In addition, Poliziano writes that "two great vices of surprisingly contrary force, were able to live together in one man: great avarice and a great desire to squander his fortune."[47] Pazzi's lust for destruction and his hatred for his city and its people as well as for his own family were such that he desired to "burn himself and his entire city in only one fire."[48] The Archbishop of Pisa, Francesco Salviati, who was another major conspirator, "despised and ignored any kind of human and divine law, participated in all murders and crimes, was lost to lechery, and had a reputation as a whoremonger."[49] Francesco Pazzi, also a conspirator, "had a characteristic peculiar to all the Pazzi family, and that is to be abnormally inclined to anger. He was short, weakly, with an olive complexion and blond hair." Moreover, it was clear "from his body language, his facial expressions and his gestures that he was a man of great insolence."[50] Jacopo Salviati, cousin of the Archbishop, "always laughed at everyone,"[51] while Jacopo Bracciolini, son of the famous Humanist Poggio Bracciolini, a former member of the Platonic Academy, a friend of the Platonic philosopher Marsilio Ficino, and a protégé of the Medici, turned to the conspiracy "because he desired new things."[52] In his attempt to explain this desire and to make his description of this conspirator comply with his stereotype of the conspirator's personality, Poliziano adds that Jacopo Bracciolini had squandered his father's fortune and was in debt. By offering greed as an explanation for Bracciolini's participation in the conspiracy, Poliziano is actually distorting history for the sake of literary effect. Jacopo Bracciolini had in fact become closer to the conspirators' group because, shortly before the conspiracy, he had obtained the position of secretary to Cardinal Raffaele Riario Sansoni, who was studying in Pisa under the protection of the Archbishop Francesco Salviati.

Poliziano's character portrayal of the participants in the Pazzi conspiracy continues, but the fundamental traits through which the author depicts their personalities are already quite clear. They are all evil people, possessed by passions and vices over which they have no control. They are closer to madness than to normality and resemble animals rather than human beings. By describing the conspirators like this, Poliziano reduces to the absurd the action in which they were involved, implying that only a group of crazed people could have desired to kill the Medici rulers. This is the same literary strategy used by Sallust in his work against Catiline. Obviously, Sallust was pro-Caesarean and Poliziano pro-Medicean.

Another element of Poliziano's description of the conspirator's personality deserves attention—his portrayal of a conspirator like Jacopo Pazzi as being torn by two opposing and contradictory passions such as avarice and prodigality. Poliziano also shares this literary trait with Sallust. They describe the conspirator as similar to a monster with the nonhuman ability to harmonize and combine in his psyche two powerful, opposing, and different forces. The conspirator is torn and strives for the exceptional act as if to give final expression to the chronic condition of moral and practical paralysis caused by a divided will. Brutus and Hamlet, two Shakespearean characters involved in conspiracies, seem to share some of the features of Poliziano's conspirators.

Poliziano's characterization of the conspirator's personality, though not the only negative one from the Renaissance, is probably the most complete and poignant. Poliziano was very close to Lorenzo de' Medici and his family and believed in the political order they had established. Consequently, he regarded anyone who would try to overthrow their rule as a conspirator, someone trying to destroy an effective form of government.

Republicanism and anti-Medicean feelings were all but dead during and following Poliziano's times, but not all authors who wrote about conspiracies were in favor of the principality. There was a line of thought in which the conspirator was the tyrannicide, the hero who fights for the freedom of the city. Niccolo' Machiavelli best represents this line of thought, which may appear quite surprising if only *The Prince* is considered. *The Prince* is indeed the political treatise in which Machiavelli justifies any action made by the ruler in order to keep his rule and any action by the would-be ruler made in order to obtain power. Machiavelli, under great emotional stress due to his recent exile from his city, wrote *The Prince* in 1513 at a critical moment in Italian politics. In it Machiavelli called for extreme remedies to an extremely serious situation. However, Machiavelli remained a populist and a republican to the end of his life, which is very obvious from all his works but *The Prince*. While Machiavelli refers to tyrannicide in his treatise on the Italian language, the *Discorso o Dialogo intorno alla nostra lingua*, where Dante is criticized, among other things, for his treatment of the figure of Brutus,[53] his ideas on the killing of the tyrant are more extensively developed in his meditation on Roman history, the *Discorsi sopra la prima deca di Tito Livio*. In a paragraph that precedes his long chapter on conspiracies, Machiavelli may be indirectly referring to Poliziano's treatment of the Pazzi plot and to his modeling of the Pazzi conspirators on Sallust's Catiline when he writes:

> And let no one be deceived about Caesar's glory, exalted as it was by writers; those who praised Caesar were corrupted by his fortune and feared his long rule which, relying on Imperial power, did not allow writers to speak freely of him. If you want

to know what free writers would have written about him, read what they wrote about Catiline. And Caesar is so much more to be execrated because he who did an evil is more to be execrated than he who wanted to do one. Consider also all the praises with which writers celebrated Brutus, because, being unable to condemn Caesar because of his power, they celebrated his enemy.[54]

Machiavelli uses the name of Caesar here both in its historical meaning and its symbolic one. It stands for the Julius Caesar who was killed by Brutus and also for the very institution of the Roman Empire; Caesar's successors, in fact, always used the name *Caesar* to identify their role and position. Machiavelli implies that a type of historical censorship took place with the birth of the Empire that prevented historians from freely writing about the emperors. He seems to identify in Sallust a primary example of this type of historiography and indicates that what Sallust wrote about Catiline he should have written about Caesar. This passage also possibly contains an indirect reference to Poliziano's analysis of the Pazzi conspiracy and to his censure of the conspirators modeled on Sallust. In this respect Machiavelli's position could not be more distant from that of Poliziano's. While the latter was a follower of the Medici, the former remained always faithful to his republican and populist ideals.

In his book on Roman history, the *Discorsi*, which is also a comparison between ancient and modern history and an attempt to understand contemporary events through the eyes of ancient historians dealing with the happenings of their own times, Machiavelli has a long chapter on conspiracies. While not everyone has the opportunity to openly wage war against a prince, Machiavelli says at the beginning of his chapter that everyone has the opportunity to start a conspiracy against him. However, conspiracies involve many dangers and history teaches that very few of them have been totally successful: "The dangers, as I have already said, that one encounters in conducting a conspiracy are great and accompany you through time: because you run into danger in the preparation, in the execution and following the execution."[55] The entire chapter, which reads a little like a manual for the perfect conspiracy, attempts to explain how these dangers can be overcome. Secrecy, Machiavelli says, is of crucial importance; thus the best conspiracies are those conducted by one or a few persons. These persons must, in addition, be courageous and determined members of the prince's entourage. Weak individuals or those who do not know the habits of the prince should not attempt to kill him. They would not have the necessary knowledge of his routine or the support to bring about their plan. The court is the only place to start a conspiracy that has some possibility of success, a reality that leads Machiavelli to expose one of his pessimistic, typically Machiavellian beliefs: "A Prince who wants to be safe from the danger of conspiracies must mistrust both those upon which he has bestowed favors and those he has persecuted: because the latter are totally deprived of means and the former abound with them; but the desire is similar, because the desire to dominate is just as big if not bigger than the desire to take revenge."[56]

Determination and swiftness are two other necessary attributes of successful conspirators. Once the decision is made, the conspirators should not retract or postpone, which would only allow time for doubts to grow and for suspicion to spread. Obviously, Machiavelli concludes, the killing is an absolute obligation in a successful conspiracy. A conspiracy which fails in its goal, such as the Pazzi conspiracy, has disastrous consequences for its perpetrators.

The greater part of Machiavelli's chapter on conspiracies displays an unusual interest in dissecting the various ingredients of the successful conspiracy. His writing reads like that of a pragmatist gone mad, one who wants accomplishments no matter how bloody the result. Machiavelli's is obviously the writing of an embittered politician, one who has transfered his political delusions to the area of political theory.

One cannot, however, explain Machiavelli's extremism without considering the situation of the Italian independent states in the sixteenth century. Their vulnerability to foreign domination justified Machiavelli's line of thought. Machiavelli says comparatively little about the motivations for or philosophies of a conspiracy. He does, however, say that princes who are hated run a greater risk of being targets of attempts against their lives than those who are loved, and that the former should try to kill their enemies before their enemies kill them. Machiavelli sets forth two motivations for the genesis of a conspiracy: hatred for the prince and the desire to return the state to freedom. As an example of the latter he quotes Brutus' conspiracy. He concludes, however, that a plot against a prince loved by his subjects is a worthless one: "Caesar is the example, who, because he enjoyed the friendship of the Romans, was vindicated by them; in fact, the Roman people having expelled the conspirators from Rome, they were indirectly responsible for the killing of all of them, at different times and in different places."[57]

The Pazzi conspiracy also stimulated the composition of a lengthy philosophical dialogue on the meaning of liberty with very strong anti-Medicean overtones. Written by Alamanno Rinuccini, a descendant of a family involved for generations in Florentine political affairs and a firm believer in the old republican ideals, the dialogue *De Libertate (On Liberty)* met with little literary success. Although it was written in 1479, the year following the Pazzi conspiracy, *De Libertate* was never republished until modern times, maybe because of its anti-Medicean bias. This alone should be a sufficient indication of the power of the Medici and of the long-lasting effects of the myth that surrounded them. Extremely well versed in both the Latin and the Greek classics and knowledgeable of ancient political theories, Rinuccini combines several different themes in the *De Libertate*. He discusses various philosophies of freedom, makes comparisons between ancient and modern history, defends his own political position in relation to the events of his time, and sharply attacks the Medici family, especially the undisputed leader of Florence, Lorenzo de' Medici. On the other hand, Alamanno Rinuccini's Stoic attitude and his need to justify his political inaction give him away. Euleutherius— the name under which Rinuccini expresses his ideas in the *De Libertate*—holds very radical views about freedom and believes that human freedom is similar to animal freedom. However, when reproached for no longer participating in Florentine politics, he justifies himself by saying that he found in the freedom offered by philosophical meditation a higher level of existence. By giving such an answer, Alamanno Rinuccini appears similar to many members of the old Roman republican aristocracy at the time of Caesar's ascent to power who declined to take up the challenge of the new political situation. Such a similarity is surprising in a work like the *De Libertate*, in which Lorenzo de' Medici is presented as the worst villain and the Pazzi conspirators as the new freedom fighters, on equal footing with the classical examples of Brutus and Cassius.

Alamanno Rinuccini is representative of the general mood affecting the old Florentine aristocracy as the Medici consolidated their firm grip on the city. Most of the aristocracy sensed the inevitability of the destiny that the city was facing and realized that, although the city was about to be deprived of its great freedom and individual liberties, history was pushing in that direction. The only choice for the old, learned, and classically minded aristocracy was to take refuge in the world of literature by believing, with a touch of resigned pessimism, that the lost political freedom could be compensated by achieving total freedom of the soul. Unlike Brutus, who appears in Plutarch constantly torn between *vita activa* (action) and *vita comtemplativa* (the cultivation of the mind), Alamanno Rinuccini seems to have given up any hope in the possibilities of action.

Such hopelessness and despair are deeply rooted in a vision of the old Florentine institutions as inevitably destined to decadence that appears more and more frequently among Florentine intellectuals and aristocrats at the end of the fifteenth century and into the sixteenth century. This vision brings with it a sense of withdrawal and noncommitment and indicates that history is uncontrollable or that its control is escaping the reach of those who held it in earlier, more felicitous times. This feeling, present in a contradictory and complex way in Niccolo' Machiavelli, will find its most noble and dramatic expression in one of his followers, the aristocratic, cynical, and pessimistic Francesco Guicciardini, who preached indifference to external events in favor of the cultivation of the *particolare*, the private realm belonging to the individual, to his family, and to his soul.

In the *De Libertate* this feeling of decadence and corruption of the traditional Florentine republican institutions is expressed in a long speech that traces the history of the Florentine Republic system back to its origins. The speech is made by the second most important character in the dialogue, Alitheus, a name derived from the Greek word for truth, *aletheia*. As such, Alitheus represents the classical and eternally valid principle of civic life:

> You are forcing me, gentlemen, to recount something which is not only difficult to tell but painful to remember, and which I cannot retell without crying. I am ashamed that I was born in my city in these times, when I see the people who once dominated a great part of the Etruscan land and either neighboring provinces being pushed here and there by the whims of an adolescent. Many men famous for their knowledge, their age, and their prudence are oppressed by the yoke of servitude, and yet as soon as they realize that they themselves have brought around servitude they do not dare to take revenge, and what is even worse, they are then forced to oppose and fight those who oppose servitude. Therefore I cannot doubt that the customs of our times have degenerated so much from those of our

ancestors that if they were to come to life again they would deny that we belong to the same people. This is because they founded, maintained, and aggrandized this Republic with the best customs, the most sacred laws and institutions tailored for the good life. Who in fact would not believe that the old laws of our city were equal if not superior to those of Lycurgus, Solon, Numa, and of all of those others who made laws and institutions tailored to the people's freedom?[58]

Alitheus paints a very bleak picture of the Florentine situation under the Medici. He describes the city as vilified by the other Italian states, deprived of freedom of speech, and controlled by a handful of greedy, arrogant, incompetent men who serve the ruler. In the dialogue, Lorenzo de' Medici is openly called a tyrant by Euleutherius, the character representing the author. This definition, however, does not lead to any important conclusions or decisions to take action. Rinuccini seems to be resigned to a situation that cannot be corrected, and maybe the failure of the Pazzi conspiracy, a conspiracy that he nevertheless praises, confirms his conviction. Indirectly, the entire dialogue can be seen as an attempt to grant philosophical dignity to resignation and passivity. Rinuccini as Euleutherius explains that he has chosen *vita contemplativa* over *vita activa* because the situation does not leave him space for constructive participation. He expresses a sentiment that will become much more widespread in the early cinquecento, when the life of the soul and of the mind will increasingly become personal alternatives to a hopeless political situation. In his pessimistic words of withdrawal, Rinuccini also expresses the signs of the end of his social class. Lorenzo de' Medici was to the Florentine aristocracy what Caesar was to the Roman senate. From a more universal point of view, in any time, age, and condition, withdrawal, for whatever reason and in the name of whatever noble principle, seems to inevitably cause the loss of political power and bring about a change at the head of the state.

Lorenzo de' Medici died in 1492 at the age of forty-three, bringing to an end an era of peace, prosperity, tranquility, and political balance for the entire Italian peninsula. After his death, Machiavelli wrote, "those seeds flourished . . . which ruined and continue to ruin Italy":

And never had anyone died, not only in Florence but in all of Italy, who was so well known as a prudent man and whose death was more mourned by his country. And the heaven sent very clear signs that after his death were to come great ruins; among them, the top of the pinnacle of the temple of Santa Reparata was hit so violently by lightning that most of it fell down, to the great amazement and astonishment of everyone.[59]

Lorenzo was succeeded by his indecisive and weak son, Piero, who was dethroned in 1494 by the religious fanatic Girolamo Savonarola; in the same year Italy was invaded by the troops of the French king Charles VIII, thus beginning the long history of Italian colonization by foreign powers. Savonarola, with French support, was able to expel the Medici from the rule of the city. He remained in power long after the French left Italy; in 1498 he was burned at the stake in the central piazza of Florence for having refused to voluntarily walk through fire in order to prove the divine inspiration of his gift of prophecy. The Republic lasted until 1512, when the younger son of Lorenzo de' Medici and the brother of Pope Leo X, Giuliano de' Medici, with the support of the Holy League, the powerful league of states originally formed by Pope Julius II, regained control of the city for himself and his family. The Medici remained in control, practically without interruption save a brief three years between 1527 and 1530, until 1737. However, a year after he had regained power, Giuliano was the object of a failed assassination attempt. The conspirators, Pietro Paolo Boscoli and Agostino Capponi, were duly arrested and condemned to death. The night preceding the execution, Luca della Robbia, a Florentine scholar, visited Pietro Paolo Boscoli and recorded their conversation in a beautifully dramatic narrative.[60] In it Boscoli, faced with death and obsessed with the Brutus myth, appears as he tries to achieve eternal salvation by dying in the grace of God. Despite his deeply held convictions, Boscoli is forced to believe by the religious culture of his times that the conspiracy in which he has participated is against God's will because the Medici rule is willed by God. Boscoli calls for a confessor to whom he can disclose all his sins, but since his usual confessor is not in Florence on that night, the better part of the narrative is a conversation between Boscoli and della Robbia. Boscoli finds it difficult to be relieved of his sins because rationally he does not understand why he has erred by following the example of Brutus in trying to free his city from its dictator. But he understands that to reach salvation he must submit his rationality to the higher, more mysterious, truth of faith:

> Then he said: Please, Luca, take Brutus out of my head, so that I may go through this totally as a Christian.

And I Luca della Robbia said: It is easy to die as a Christian. And you know that those Roman things have not been written truthfully, but have been artfully aggrandized.

So he said: And even if they were true, what good are they to me if they do not bring about the desired result?

And I: Here you are, you are healed with your own words.

And he: Luca, do not praise me.

And I: I am here to help you. Tell me what you need because I am encouraged if I, with God's help, can be of comfort: or, rather, you will comfort me.

And he: My intellect believes in the faith and wants me to die as a Christian, but I feel that I am forcing it. And I think that I have a hard heart. I don't know if I'm making my idea clear.

And I: I understand it. You would like to have an easy understanding of God, with tears and sobbing, and you would like your intellect to embrace the faith spontaneously.

And he: Yes, that is it.

And I: Pietro Paolo, the second thing is not necessary for salvation, but you must have the first one. You must force your intellect and submit it to faith. And soon it will seem to you that you are not forcing it. And thus you will have tears, because you will have the help of confession, communion, indulgences and the prayers of those who are present. Have no doubts: concentrate all your desires in God, because God says: *fili, praebe mihi cor tuum* [my son, give me your heart].[61]

Unable to live like a Roman, Boscoli is trying to die like a Christian. The task is more difficult than it would seem, however, because the Christian faith seems to be more a necessity brought about by the fear of the immediacy of death than by a deeply felt conviction. In *Political Murder: From Tyrannicide to Terrorism*, a comprehensive study of tyrannicide from its beginnings to modern times, Franklin L. Ford writes that Boscoli's uncertainties express "the interplay of Christian and classical ideals in the fantasies of a Renaissance tyrannicide."[62] While this is undoubtedly true, the Boscoli episode signifies much more. Rinuccini's dialogue *De Libertate* reveals the position of a disillusioned and disheartened Florentine republican of the old ruling class who, having realized that the control of the political situation is no longer in his hands, decides to reform his life. He abandons political activity (*vita activa*) and reaches for higher and more universal truth in the world of philosophical meditation and ideas (*vita contemplativa*). In Luca della Robbia's description of Pietro Paolo Boscoli's death, this evolution is carried a step further. Unlike Rinuccini, Boscoli did indeed try to act, to bring back the republican order by conspiring against the prince. Infatuated with the old Roman ideals and holding Brutus as the supreme model, he conducted a conspiracy against Giuliano de' Medici. Unlike Brutus, however, Boscoli failed, which shattered his faith in the classical ideals and in the Brutus myth. As a consequence of his act he is condemned to die; his execution finds the approval of a different faith, the Christian one, which supports the state. When a confessor finally arrives a few hours before the execution to listen to Boscoli's sins so that he may gain eternal salvation, Luca della Robbia recommends that the confessor tell Boscoli that "Saint Thomas says that these conspiracies are not legitimate."[63] In della Robbia's view, the quotation of one of the Church's major philosophical authorities may help Boscoli to embrace the true faith, thus dying like a Christian, ashamed of his act, rather than like a Roman, proud of it.

Della Robbia's narration of Boscoli's death could, however, be interpreted from a more metaphorical point of view and be seen as a step in the development of sixteenth-century political theory and social morality. In 1513, the year of Boscoli's execution, the term *ragion di stato* (reason of state) had not yet been created, but it will be created shortly thereafter as a direct outcome of the Florentine political situation. *Ragion di stato,* the idea that any act by the state, whether considered moral or immoral, just or unjust, fair or unfair, is justified on the basis of the state's superior reasons for self-preservation, places the decision-making process exclusively in the hands of the ruler. Individual citizens are not allowed to make judgments about this idea, as only the rulers can know all the reasons and motivations for which a decision is made. As such, the individual citizen has no right to judge, let alone to try to kill the prince. Every element in the political body must coalesce to support and justify the state, especially religion; religion has the power to threaten with eternal damnation the individual who is found guilty against the state. And through religion, presumably the highest possible moral system, Boscoli is forced to believe exactly the opposite of what he would normally believe if allowed to think with his own mind. While he would believe that to kill the prince is the greatest good for the state, he is forced to believe that it is the worst evil and that he must atone and willfully accept death for having tried to do so. Luca della

Robbia's description of how Boscoli finally decides to accept his death does not end with Boscoli's full submission, however. After the confession is over, Boscoli asks the friar:

> Help me die for the love of Christ. I would like to face death without any doubts, with so much faith that it could annihilate reason. But I feel a war inside of me that bothers me more than death, because I am ready to die.
>
> So the Friar said to him: Look, my brother, this war that you feel inside you will have it to the last moment; and no Christian, no matter how saintly in his own right, can free himself of it. But we must win over it: because even Jesus Christ felt this contradiction between feeling and reason, and in overcoming it lies our victory. . . .
>
> I want you to die for the love of Christ and nothing else, except that you should know that your sins deserve this and much worse.[64]

Boscoli should be grateful, his confessor is saying, that he is being executed and that he will find eternal salvation. His sin, attempting to take the life of the prince, would indeed deserve a much more severe punishment. No statement could be used to more clearly indicate the cultural and political climate of the time. The would-be murderer of a totalitarian ruler in a city of ancient republican traditions is asked to be grateful for having been enlightened about the gravity of his crime. He is asked to do so in the name of eternity and of salvation after death. In almost one hundred years, from the beginning of the fifteenth century to the second decade of the sixteenth century, the civic ideas of republican life and of freedom have become dead issues. Faced with international problems larger than itself, Italy, divided into many states, survives through absolute power and the power of the Church. God's earthly representative, the Roman pontiff, with destiny and salvation firmly under his control, can still play for Italy in the European power game. Let the Medici speak to the pope and let the pope speak to the king of France. In this chain of command the ethics of Italian politics will play themselves out and the results will be, at least initially, tragic.

Lorenzino de' Medici: A New Brutus

Although destiny opposed his reputation and his legacy, the Brutus myth survived stronger than ever at the Medici court in the city of Florence. Now a ducal dynasty with two popes—Leo X and Clement VII—from their family, the protection of the Holy Roman Emperor, and the 1533 marriage of Catherine de' Medici and the duke d'Orleans, who would later become the king of France as Henry II, the Medici enjoyed a seemingly untouchable standing in European politics in the first half of the sixteenth century. Perhaps to confirm the irony of Machiavelli's *Prince*, finally published in 1532, that the ruler has to fear the most threats to his life from the inner circle of power and especially from members of his family, Lorenzo de' Medici, also called Lorenzino or Lorenzaccio, killed the duke Alessandro de' Medici in a murder that had the number six as its fearful omen. The duke was twenty-six years of age, the date was 6 January 1537 (actually 1536 according to the old Florentine calendar), and at six o'clock that morning the victim was stabbed six times. Lorenzino, as he was commonly called (which distinguishes him from the other Lorenzo de' Medici, Lorenzo the Magnificent), was the son of Pierfrancesco de' Medici and Maria Soderini. He was born in Florence in 1514, the offspring of a decayed and impoverished branch of the illustrious family. Historians and scholars remember him as the killer of the duke, certainly as the most famous tyrannicide of Renaissance history and literature. Lorenzino shares with Brutus and Hamlet the fame of the great tyrannicides and chronologically stands between them, almost symbolizing that his myth belongs as much to history as it does to literature.

He has the historical presence of the tyrannicide whose life was recorded in city documents and whose actions were witnessed and examined by many. But with Hamlet, the quintessential literary character, Lorenzino shares certain enigmatic qualities. An intellectual who turned to action, Lorenzino probably willfully tried to spite the court and people of his own times by making his act a mystery. No one ever knew why he killed the duke, which is the source of his literary success and the reason why historians and writers periodically revive his myth. Unlike Hamlet, who expresses on the stage his doubts, ambiguities, and uncertainties about the course of action to be taken, Lorenzino's enigmatic qualities are frozen on the pages of historical facts. He hardly ever spoke for himself, except for a brief and puzzling *Apologia* (*Apology*) that he wrote after his act to justify it. Lorenzino does not participate in the questioning and the probing of his personality, a role that has been taken on entirely by his interpreters. Many major historians, artists, and scholars have been intrigued with and have written about Lorenzino, starting with some of his great contemporaries such as Michelangelo, Benvenuto Cellini, and the Florentine historian Benedetto Varchi and ending with the contemporary avant-garde actor-playwrite Carmelo Bene. In the introduction to his play on Lorenzino modeled after Alfred de Musset's *Lorenzaccio,* Carmelo Bene sees Lorenzino's act against the duke as committed simply to prove his ability to revive the historical role of the tyrannicide. According to Bene, the mystery of Lorenzino's act is paradoxically explained precisely by its mystery. It is a meaningless act, one committed only to justify gratuitous action:

> Lorenzaccio needed an act which would free him once and for all from being free to will and to understand. Once and for all, a meta-historical and extralinguistic act. He didn't know what to do with reality, with private and public life, with untrustworthy friends, with love of love, and with country. So why not reinvent the discredited myth of the tyrant? Why not reinvent that obsolete story and finally strike the void at its heart? So that the misinterpreting of a "noble" or "ignoble" cause would not interfere with the "getting even" between the two sides of his self, and would not be declassified to the lower status of real action.[65]

The account of Lorenzino from which most other stories have been taken was told by the Florentine historian Benedetto Varchi in his monumental work *Storia Fiorentina (Florentine History).* From him we learn that Lorenzino spent his youth in Rome at the court of Clement VII, the second Medici pope, who loved him dearly. However, little else is known about Lorenzino's Roman years except that he took active part in all the fanfare, the enjoyments, and probably the intrigues of the papal court. He relished the company of prostitutes and was said to have experimented with homosexuality, an inclination that was so fashionable that the pope was said to have practiced it. Most of all, Lorenzino's Roman years were years of education during which he read and became fascinated with the classics. From knowledge of this education, history has a claim to Lorenzino as a man of letters, not of action. Maybe the two are not contradictory. As he was living in the papal court and witnessing the intrigues, the treacheries, and the injustices of the Roman political institution sumptuously living its last years of glory before the ensuing decadence, Lorenzino was also meditating on the great Romans of classical times who opposed corruption and decadence. Perhaps at this time the myth and image of Brutus took shape in Lorenzino's mind as the great liberator, the citizen who wants to reinstate order.

From Rome Lorenzino had to return to Florence in 1530 because one night in May of the same year while he walked with a group of friends to the Arch of Constantine, as if possessed by sudden madness, he destroyed the statues of the Roman emperors that decorated the illustrious monument. This first meaningless act did not encounter the tolerance of the pope, who ordered an immediate arrest of the vandals. Lorenzino, however, had already left Rome and was safe in Florence, the city that was going to offer his sword not statues but real flesh. Speculation on the meaning of Lorenzino's attack of the statues is futile other than to call it an attempt to display power—by destroying the very symbols of ancient power—on the part of a powerless individual. The act reveals a flawed character, described by Benedetto Varchi in terms that remind us both of Sallust's description of Catiline and of Poliziano's analysis of the Pazzi conspirators:

> As soon as he had left the custody of his mother and of his teacher he started displaying a soul incapable of peace, insatiable and inclined to evil, and shortly thereafter, under the guidance of Filippo Strozzi, he started ridiculing all things, both human and divine; he associated mainly with lowly people, who would respect him and agree with him in all things, rather than with his peers. He indulged in all pleasures, especially those of lust, without distinction of sex, age, condition, and while he apparently flattered everyone he didn't respect anyone: he tried to acquire glory in an awkward way, and he didn't say or do one thing without believing that it would increase his fame as a gallant or as a witty man. Physically he was very thin, or rather emaciated, and this is why he was called Lorenzino. He never smiled and laughed in a sinister way, and with his dark and melancholic face he was of graceful looks rather than handsome. Nevertheless in his youth he was greatly loved by Pope Clement, although (as he himself said after killing the Duke Alexander) he was ready to kill him.[66]

Benedetto Varchi's portrait of Lorenzino does not even try to conceal its many literary references; Varchi clearly attributes the murder of the duke to the murderer's complex, bizarre, and ultimately monstrous personality. We get an image of Lorenzino as the evil and sinister hero, flawed both mentally and physically, unable to have feelings and emotions, and constantly second-guessing to outsmart his friends. His lustful nature and need to associate with lowly people add color to the picture, while his inclination towards literature and history—which gained him the name of *filosofo* (philosopher)—appears to be interpreted partly as a disguise and partly as a feature that adds to his mental confusion. Lorenzino's incomprehensible destruction of the Roman statues is therefore put on the same level with the killing of the duke; both are meaningless and aimless acts committed simply for the fame and renown that he was unable to acquire in other more noble and constructive ways. True, many republicans with strong anti-Medicean feelings who might have looked positively at an attempt against the duke remained either in Florence or in exile to other cities. However, Lorenzino's relationship with the members of this largely exiled republican party, dreamers about a political condition that history had made obsolete, is hardly documented. Reports of Lorenzino's dealings with some republicans exist, but these dealings were probably made to spy on the duke's enemies and to keep the ruler of Florence well-informed on their activities.[67] Lorenzino was a great dissimulator. He was the duke's closest friend and his regular companion in frequent escapades in search of women and fun during many dark Florentine nights. Lorenzino's dissimulation was perfectly contrived and never revealed. One is almost led to think that he acted against the duke with such planned perfection to prove that Machiavelli, who believed that murder attempts against the ruler conducted by only one man were practically impossible, was wrong: "Of those souls of men willing to conduct a conspiracy by themselves, I believe one can find many who would like to do it, but very few who actually do do it. And of those who do it there are very few or none who do not get killed immediately after the act: and one does not find anyone who wants to encounter a sure death."[68] Did Lorenzino kill the duke to prove that the impossible is actually possible? Was his act a philosophical one intended to demonstrate that destiny can be challenged? The latter is probably the correct explanation, but the other possible, yet very remote, explanation, periodically raised in the literature on this subject, is that Lorenzino acted on behalf of the king of France, who wanted the duke killed because he had married the daughter of Emperor Charles V. Moreover, Lorenzino, as an intelligent observer of his times, must have known that the republican party had no chance to regain control of the city and that the dead duke would be immediately replaced with a new, probably more cruel and tyrannical, one.

Another contemporary of Lorenzino and an intelligent observer of the events of his own times, the Florentine historian Francesco Guicciardini is reported to have commented that by killing the duke Lorenzino obtained three things that he did not want. He lost his best friend, made an enemy of Cosimo de' Medici, Alessandro's successor, and ultimately strengthened the Medici rule over Florence. He did, however, execute a perfect plot and gain for himself a page—as inglorious as it may have turned out to be—in the history of Italy, and these are probably the two things he wanted more than any others. Had he not killed the duke probably only a footnote here and there would speak of him as the duke's panderer, but with the murder Lorenzino acquired the dubious glory of being remembered as the most famous of the new Brutuses.

History certainly owes Lorenzino at least a mention as the perfect plotter. Despite posthumous affirmations to the contrary and some reports of predictions by seers and visionaries, no one was really able to see through Lorenzino's perfect dissimulation. After the duke was killed, two major sixteenth-century figures had claims to the contrary. The artist Benvenuto Cellini, himself in Florence in 1535 escaping Roman justice for killing a man, was called to make a portrait of the duke on a medal. In his *Vita* (*Autobiography*), which Cellini started composing over twenty years after Alessandro de' Medici's death, the artist thus describes one of his meetings with the Florentine ruler and Lorenzino, both of whom are trying to convince him not to leave the city and to finish his work:

> And present at these conversations was the said Lorenzino de' Medici and no one else. And many times the Duke made a sign to him so that he too would convince me to stay on. And that Lorenzino said nothing but: "Benvenuto, it would be better for you to stay." And to this I answered that I wanted by all means to return to Rome. And he did not say anything else, and was always staring at the Duke with a sinister look. I, having finished the medal in my own way and having locked it in his drawer, said to the Duke: "Sir, be at peace that I will make a much more beautiful medal than I did for Pope Clement. Reason says that I will do a better one, since the other one [the one for the Pope] was the first one I ever did. And Lorenzo here will give me a beautiful idea for the subject matter of the reverse side of the medal, as he is a very learned and ingenious man." And to this the said Lorenzo immediately answered by saying:

"I wasn't thinking about anything else but to give a reverse side worthy of his excellency." The Duke chuckled, looked at Lorenzo, and said: "Lorenzo, you will give him the reverse and he will do it here without leaving." And Lorenzo quickly answered: "I will do it as soon as possible, and I hope to do something that will amaze the world." The Duke, who thought of him [Lorenzino] at times as a little crazy and at times as very lazy, turned in his bed and laughed about what he had said.[69]

With this report full of innuendo and double entendre, Cellini possibly tried to claim a foresight that no one actually could claim. The "reverse" side of the medal representing the portrait of the duke Alessandro for which Lorenzino is to find an idea appears therefore as a reversal of the duke's life, a happening that will "amaze the world."

Similarly, Giorgio Vasari, the architect, painter, and biographer of artists, also alleges that Lorenzino's intentions could have been anticipated. In his biography of the architect Bastiano da San Gallo, who in 1536 worked with Lorenzino in Florence at the special staging of Lorenzino's comedy *Aridosia*, written in celebration of the marriage of the duke Alessandro and Margaret of Absburg, daughter of Charles V, Vasari says that Lorenzino, "who was always thinking of how to kill the Duke," wanted the stage to be built in such a way that it would crash on the duke and other members of the audience and kill them all.[70] In fact, this wish is not confirmed by any other contemporary source and may very well be a fantasy of Vasari's. In writing after the duke's death he may have wanted the glory of offering some post factum insight into a murder that no one in Italy had been able to anticipate.

Not even Lorenzino in his *Apologia* (*Apology*)—the short tract the exile in Venice wrote not long before his murder was avenged with his assassination by a Medici emissary in 1548—was able to explain the reasons for his act. If anything, the *Apologia* clouds the issue even more. It takes for granted that Alessandro was a tyrant who deserved to be killed and is intended as a plea of innocence to the many accusations of which Lorenzino had become a target. After briefly dismissing Alessandro's tyranny by saying that he was worse than the Roman emperors Nero and Caligula, Lorenzino also tries to dismiss the frequent accusation that he killed a relative and betrayed a friend who trusted him entirely. As to his blood relationship to Alessandro, Lorenzino refers to the law for his support:

That he [Alessandro] was not of the Medici family and a relative
of mine is well known, because he was born of a woman of very
lowly and vulgar condition from Colle Vecchio near Rome, who
was a lowly servant of the Duke Lorenzo and was married to a
coachman, and all the above is very well documented. There
are doubts whether the Duke Lorenzo at that time in which he
was exiled had anything to do with this servant; and if he did
it happened no more than once. But who is so ignorant of the
customs of men and of the law who doesn't know that when a
man has a wife and he is with her, even if she sins and exposes
her body to everyone's libido, all the children that she has are
always judged as being, and actually are, of the husband, as the
law always tries to preserve morality as much as it can.[71]

In addressing the second accusation that he is a traitor and the
killer of his best friend and protector, Lorenzino claims that Alessandro never trusted or loved him. The duke "never allowed me to carry
arms and always kept me disarmed as he did with the other citizens,
all of whom he suspected."[72] The weakest point of the *Apologia* is,
however, Lorenzino's explanation of his goals following Alessandro's
death. This long and at times convoluted part of his justification also
answers the numerous accusations that were raised against him, all
of which involved the inconclusiveness of Alessandro's murder, an
act without finality enacted simply for the act itself. In a sentence with
a clear Machiavellian flavor Lorenzino tries to deny the accusation: "I
say therefore that my goal was to free Florence; and the killing of the
Duke was the means."[73]

Lorenzino goes on to say that he decided to keep his plan absolutely
secret to be sure that the plot would not be uncovered and subsequently aborted. He claims that in the city the anti-Medicean party
had been weakened and the opposition largely broken, and that it
would therefore have been extremely risky to publicize the murder
in Florence even after its execution. His intention was to come back
to Florence after Alessandro's death with the members of the exiled
anti-Medicean party "who were well armed,"[74] rather than try to
incite a rebellion among the people in the city, who were in great
part accustomed to tyranny. Lorenzino claims—a dubious claim after
having so strongly defended the secrecy of his plot—that those who
criticized his conduct following Alessandro's death should have ad-
vised him earlier. While realizing and admitting that his plot did not
achieve its goal, Lorenzino is not willing to take the blame entirely.

Rather, he blames the Florentine exiles for not following his call and not attempting to liberate the city. The conclusion of the *Apologia*, in which Lorenzino claims the glory due to heroes, may be the most revealing part of the entire work. Unwilling to accept a dubious page in history, Lorenzino sets himself apart from the rest of the world. To justify his place in posterity, Lorenzino openly says that the final failure of his act was caused exclusively by the inability of all others to act:

> For all these reasons I can sooner claim to have freed Florence—having left her without a tyrant—than they [the Florentine exiles] can claim that I have done something wrong. Because not only did I kill the tyrant, but I myself went to call and solicit all those that I knew could, and that I thought would want to, do more than others for the freedom of their city. And is it my fault if I didn't find them ready and willing as they should have been?[75]

Despite his passionate, although problematic, self-defense, history has not been generous to Lorenzino, who is most often remembered by the disparaging name of Lorenzaccio. Indeed, his plot against the duke, conducted as it was in great secrecy and without any preparation for political decisions after the murder, has generally been considered as a futile and meaningless act. In fact, it achieved the result opposite to the one for which Lorenzino claimed it was intended: it strengthened the Medici rule over the city and eliminated any possibility of rebellion. With Lorenzino's failure all hopes of restoring Florence to republican rule died forever.

The question then remains: why did Lorenzino do it? Why did he attempt such a dangerous act while probably knowing that no practical results would come from it? If no answer to this question can be found in history, if events as they were remembered by witnesses and recorded by historians do not offer any plausible explanation for Lorenzino's act, then our explanation must be found in the psyche of Lorenzino himself. To explore this angle a good place to start is in Benvenuto Cellini's passing comment that the duke Alessandro considered Lorenzino "a little crazy." More recent writers, availing themselves of the terminology and the insight of psychology, interpreted Lorenzino's craziness and determination in killing the duke as a sort of mania stemming from the need to excel through that act, since every other possibility to glory was precluded to him. Born into an impoverished branch of a great family and having grown up and always lived in the proximity of pomp and power, both at the papal court in Rome and at the duke's court in Florence, without ever having been the center of attention, Lorenzino gained the spotlight that had always shone on someone very close to him by taking Alessandro's life. He had indirectly participated in the splendor and grandeur of the life-styles of both the pope and the duke and probably thought that his role at court had not been adequately recognized. This awareness might have been accompanied by a feeling of self-hatred or of low self-esteem. After ali, Lorenzino procured women for the duke and regularly accompanied him on frequent nightly escapades. Even on the night of the murder Lorenzino had been able to lure the duke into his bedroom by promising him the graces of his own aunt, Caterina Soderini Ginori. As a member of the Medici family, he probably thought that he deserved a better career!

According to Adolfo Borgognoni, one of Lorenzino's most accurate biographers from the nineteenth century, the precision with which he organized the murder and the perfect dissimulation with which he was able to hide from everyone his real intention are symptomatic of a folly and of a mania that go beyond normality:

> Francesco Puccinotti[76] writes that in the case of a mania, when it comes with hatred against someone, the maniac's dissimulation reaches "an extreme level." And in truth dissimulation and simulation (two things that in such occurrences are often identical) reached such a degree in Lorenzo that beyond that, I believe, it would be impossible to go. And as such, he also appears to be cold-blooded, analytical, possessing incredible lucidity in his ability to prepare all the details of his act. This latter aspect (which psychiatrists consider one of the main aspects of manias), added to the other ones already described, shows that a constant and sickly thought, fixed and unchangeable, ruled over the mind and guided the Florentine tyrannicide.[77]

Rather than remembered as a new Brutus, the Roman hero whose example he wanted to follow and whose glory he wanted to equal, Lorenzino is remembered as a man guided by maniacal passions. In his inability to plan how Florence was to regain its freedom following the duke's death—an impossibility given the political conditions of the time—lies the reason for the sinister historical portrayal of

Lorenzino. The times in which he lived and in which he brought about his plan did not favor him. Maybe history used Lorenzino, the last of the Italian Renaissance tyrannicides, to prove that tyrannicide, at least for a while, was out of style. This is perhaps also why in preparing and carrying out his plot, Lorenzino cared more about its theatrical aspects than the political ones. History, making little allowances for freedom, chose a man who was not free to act to prove that monarchical rule was impossible to challenge. Destiny and madness, both conspiring to prove the futility of the free act, seemed to devilishly plot this last heroic act, or rather its parody.

Lorenzino evokes the ghostlike memory of Brutus, wracking his disturbed mind and pushing himself to make a decision without a chance for any good end because both the intended victim and the ultimately naive perpetrator of the liberating act were destroyed. At least symbolically, this act also served as the closing chapter of one of the most glorious periods of western European history. With Florence firmly in the Medicis' hands, liberty, the force that more than any other made the Renaissance possible, was dead.

Brutus, Lorenzino, and Michelangelo

Lorenzino's murder of the duke was not immediately perceived as a failure and as a futile political act. For a short time a small hope arose among the most determined and enduring republican exiles, including Michelangelo, one of the most faithful to the idea of liberty whose hatred for the Medici reached proverbial proportions. Refusing to lose hope that freedom could return to Florence one day, he testified to this brief moment of optimism that spread among the liberal forces throughout Italy, particularly among the last hopeful Florentine republicans, by sculpting a bust of Brutus to celebrate Lorenzino's heroic act. Michelangelo was persuaded to sculpt the Brutus bust by another republican exile who was, like Michelangelo, living in Rome. Donato Giannotti, follower of Machiavelli, political theorist, and secretary of Cardinal Ridolfi, participated in political negotiations in Florence to remove Alessandro's successor, Duke Cosimo de' Medici. But hope was lost very early in the process, and upon returning to Rome in 1539, Giannotti knew that the Florentine republican cause, like Athenian democracy, could in the future be celebrated only in the arts.

Giannotti did not exhaust his worship of Brutus by convincing

Michelangelo, one of the greatest artists of those times, to sculpt the famous bust. He had also planned to write a play on Brutus, maybe the first one of the fairly rich lot that was to come later on, but the play was either never written or has been lost. Finally, several years later, probably in the middle of the 1540s, Giannotti wrote a dialogue on the Brutus myth in which Michelangelo appears as one of the main interlocutors. Interestingly, in Giannotti's dialogue, a unique document of what probably was an actual discussion on Brutus with Michelangelo and others, the Brutus topic is approached again through Dante's poem. This interpolation is extremely revealing as it shows how the republican exiles, who had been ready to actively take part in any political development in their city, were now examining their ideals through the mediation of literature. The opportunity for urgent political action is no longer present in the dialogue, and the rethinking of political ideals through the subtle, philosophical poetry of Dante offers both a consolation and a distraction from harsh realities. Like all great literature, Dante's poem functions for Giannotti and Michelangelo as a consolation for the final defeat of what had been a worthwhile and noble cause.

The discussion on Brutus takes place in the second of the two *Dialogi di Donato Giannotti de' giorni che Dante consumo' nel cercare l'Inferno e 'l Purgatorio*[78] (*Donato Giannotti's Dialogues on the Days That Dante Spent Looking Through the Inferno and Purgatory*) that, like the first dialogue, is largely dedicated to the discussion of a complex chronological and astronomical point involving Dante's *Inferno* and *Purgatory*. In the discussion, Michelangelo, said to be a great lover of Dante who enjoyed the fame of being a scholar of *The Divine Comedy*, tries to convince his friends that even the most complex astronomical points of Dante's poem are correct and that Dante left nothing to chance. Every detail in the poem, Michelangelo insists, can be explained mathematically. This idea does not convince Donato Giannotti, who exclaims that Dante was, after all, a human being and that human beings always make mistakes. When asked to give an example, Giannotti, unable to fault Dante on astronomical grounds, turns to the more familiar topic of politics and exclaims: "Don't you think that Dante made a mistake by placing Brutus and Cassius in Lucifer's mouth?"[79]

Giannotti goes on to say that Dante does not seem to know that the "universal consensus of humankind . . . celebrates, honors, and extols those who, to free their country, kill tyrants" and that the "laws of the world promise great and honored prizes, and not horrible punishments, to those who do away with tyrants."[80] Responding in defense of Dante, Michelangelo adopts the same rhetorical line with which we have become quite familiar from earlier defenders such as Leonardo Bruni and Cristoforo Landino. Michelangelo brings up the distinction that must be made between the symbolic value and the historical value of Brutus and Cassius, indicating that by punishing them in Lucifer's mouth Dante did not really want to punish the killers of Caesar:

> He [Dante] needed very famous examples, and could not find any more or equally famous than Brutus and Cassius; and he did not think that he was insulting their memory, as he did not place them in hell as Brutus and Cassius, but as examples of those who betray Imperial majesty, as represented by Caesar, without nevertheless freeing him from the infamy of having turned the state into tyranny and of being a tyrant.[81]

As the diatribe seems to settle on this popular compromise among Florentine republicans discussing the fate of Brutus and Cassius in the hands of Dante, Michelangelo's speech takes an unexpected turn. Almost contradicting what he said previously by seemingly reacting to his standard defense of Dante as being full of hypocritical common-places aimed at bringing peace between two opposing views, Michel-angelo, in a passionate conclusion, raises the possibility that Brutus and Cassius' act was wrongful:

> It is a great presumption to kill the ruler of a public administra-tion, be he just or unjust, without knowing absolutely what good will come from his death, and while there is some hope for good while he is alive. I have become tired of, and unable to bear, those who say that no good can be done if one does not begin with an evil, and that is with death; and they do not understand that times change, new situations arise, human desires also change, men get tired, so that many times, and without pain or danger for anyone, that good that was always desired comes about.[82]

What is the cause for such an abrupt change of thinking in Michelan-gelo within almost the same page of the dialogue? Just a few lines after his defense of Brutus and Cassius conducted along the allegorical lines sanctioned by tradition, in an apparent about-face, the artist implies that perhaps Caesar's "evil" was a lesser evil than the evils that followed his death. In the first part of his discussion of the two Roman liberators, Michelangelo follows the traditional Renaissance defense of the individual's right to intervention to prevent a perversion of the proper course of history. By assigning an allegorical rather than a historical meaning to Dante's punishment of Brutus and Cassius, Michelangelo, while preserving the memory of the poet, glorifies the liberators; they took upon themselves, through the exercise of their own free will, the task of redressing the crime that Caesar had committed against the Roman Republic. He expresses his Renaissance and republican belief in the individual's right to personally intervene in the affairs of the state. But in the conclusion of his speech, as he places the control of power outside of the individual's reach, Michelangelo expresses the diametrically opposite view, which is typically royalist and follows the political thinking of the Italian and the Spanish Counter-Reformation.

In his final statement Michelangelo says doubtfully that maybe people are unable to judge historical events ("times change, new situations arise") as they judge new things on the basis of past models. But Michelangelo seems to imply that what was once evil need not always be evil. At times from an apparently negative situation a good may ultimately arise if events are given a chance to develop naturally. Michelangelo, clearly contradicting himself, is saying that it may have been better if Caesar had not been killed but rather had been given a chance to bring his political program to full development. Maybe destiny, chance, providence, or some other hidden or mysterious force overlooking human history would have operated for the general good, even under the negative disguise of a dictatorship.

Conclusion

This type of historical thinking that places the duty to define the future course of human events on destiny rather than on human wisdom prevailed in Italy during the two centuries that followed the Renaissance. With an obvious analogy to Roman history, some scholars called this historical thinking Tacitean.[83] Tacitus wrote in Rome during the first century A.D. about the first Roman emperors with nostalgic feelings for the virtuous days of the Republic. His underlying historical philosophy was fatalistic; although he paid attention to individual action and motivation, the overall view of his history is dominated by destiny, a force over which humankind has little power. For Tacitus the perfect condition for Rome was the Republic, but he was also quick in pointing out that the Republic had exhausted its historical role and that destiny had called for a new political order.

What is, is what ought to be seems to be Tacitus'—and Michelangelo's—historical belief. This view of history places wisdom in a metaphysical area, unreachable by the individual, and indirectly justifies absolute power and especially monarchy based on divine will. If history is ruled by destiny, then God, and only God, knows what is politically appropriate. This historical view also justifies the prerogative of rulers to act as they wish. In fact, a seemingly evil course of action may be the highest good when examined with destiny and ultimate goals in mind. It is the triumph of *ragion di stato* (reason of state), the political philosophy that frees the ruler from any judgment outside that of God; a book by this very title, written in 1589 by the Italian Jesuit Giovanni Botero, is still today considered one of the major manifestos on the justification of absolute power.

In writing about Brutus during the first part of the seventeenth century in Spain, where more than any other country absolute power reached absolute fulfillment, the baroque writer Francisco de Quevedo said:

> It is an evil to kill any man; but to kill the king is a terrible sin and it is a terrible treason not only to lay hands on him, but also to speak of his person with little reverence, or to think of his actions with little respect. The good king must be loved; the bad one must be endured. God allows for the tyrant, as it is in his power to punish him or depose him. And will the subject, who must obey him, not allow for him [the tyrant]?
>
> God's arm does not need our knifes for his punishments, nor our hands for his revenge.[84]

Quevedo brings to extreme conclusions the type of argument presented in Michelangelo's last speech in Giannotti's *Dialogi*. This argument in support of absolute power was typical in Catholic countries during the Counter-Reformation. With the disappearance of republicanism in Florence and most other Italian states, a process that took only a few years between the end of the fifteenth century and the beginning of the sixteenth century, the Renaissance, with its philosophy of free will and its emphasis on human dignity, power, and ability to shape one's own destiny, was soon dead. Truth and destiny and good and evil became again the special and privileged territory of higher powers and of their interpreters. The Renaissance competition between humankind and God—with free will at its center—was, by and large, to play itself out more fully in cultures that inherited the Renaissance tradition and that continued to believe that destiny was, at least, an uncertain entity.

3

Brutus, Destiny, and Tragedy

The Brutus Archetype

The glorious period of the Renaissance Brutuses ends with Lorenzino's murder of the Duke of Florence and with Giannotti's dialogue. Giannotti's aborted intention to write a play on the subject and his long intellectual discussions on Dantesque literary matters are additional signs that the last Florentine republicans, pushed away from the world of politics, had time to involve themselves in such lofty endeavors. As futile as these pursuits may have been, they were all that remained for the few enduring believers in liberty. Thus, the Brutus character, after a rather short and illustrious period of active participation in the arena of human events during which his imitators took the political destiny of their cities into their own hands by holding their daggers to the hearts and throats of princes and potential tyrants, was ready to reenter the world of literature. The character returned to literature enriched and transformed, quite different from the Brutus we found in the pages of Dante or in those of his early Renaissance commentators. The actual plots that were conducted during the Renaissance and the writings about them, which always referred to the Brutus of Roman times, strengthened and enriched the legend already existing around the figure of the liberator-tyrannicide, turning it into a historical character with unalterable and established features. These features would create the great success of Brutus as a theatrical persona throughout the late French and Italian Renaissance and, later, in English Elizabethan theatre. Subsequently, these features will remain alive in the European theatre until modern times. Moreover, the stereotyping of the Brutus character and the study of the most notable aspects of his personality seem to have established some basic elements that reappear with striking frequency in psychological and historical investigations into the nature of terrorism. The Brutus archetype transmitted through time by the Renaissance is an inherently modern persona whose basic characteristics are common and recognizable in modern society.

Four recurring characteristics of Brutus' personality are easily found through the study of the Brutus myth in history, literature, and theatre. Theatre dedicated to the Brutus character in France, Italy, and England contributed greatly to establishing his basic character traits as archetypal characteristics of the rebel of our culture and, more universally, of the rebel of all times. It is not difficult to distinguish some of these most basic characteristics.

Without doubt, the first and most important element of the Brutus archetype that has emerged is that Brutus committed a parricide. Since Brutus was not the son of Caesar, the attribution of the crime of parricide acquires an important symbolic meaning. Historically, the idea that Brutus was Caesar's son probably surfaced when both were still living and was reinforced by Brutus' mother, Servilia, and Caesar being lovers (Pompeius killed her husband when Brutus was very young). The idea was furthermore fortified by the many favors that Caesar accorded to Brutus, including pardoning him after the Roman civil war during which Brutus fought against Caesar on the side of Pompeius, despite Pompeius' murder of his father. The assertion that Caesar was the father of Brutus appears with some frequency in ancient authors, starting probably with Plutarch[1] and Suetonius, the latter telling how Caesar addressed Brutus with the Greek word *teknon* (son)[2]—the first word of Sophocles' play *Oedipus the King*— as Brutus was approaching him to kill him.

Power and fatherhood, almost synonymous in archaic and primitive societies,[3] are often associated in classical and medieval history. When the historian Tacitus in the *Annals* discusses why Augustus killed Brutus and Cassius, he explains that it was because "they had killed his father."[4] However, Tacitus knew that Augustus was only the grandson of one of Caesar's sisters and was adopted by Caesar's family, the Gens Julia, when Caesar decided to make him his heir.[5] Moreover, the later deification of Caesar helped to extend this myth to that of a universal father or father of the state. This latter conception must have provided the basis for the medieval and Dantesque idea of the emperor as the earthly representative of God. The emperor, as the father of the people he rules, is similar to God.

Machiavelli, one of the most widely read and influential authors of the Renaissance, supported the idea that a prince should run his state like a father runs his family and added a tragic and dramatic element to the theme. In a chapter of book 3 of the *Discorsi*, which probably follows similar statements in Aristotle's *Politics*[6] and is appropriately titled "Delle Congiure" ("On Plots"), Machiavelli insistently repeats that the prince should always be on guard against assassination attempts, especially coming from those "who are the most familiar" with him.[7] For Machiavelli only those who are closest to the prince and know him best can reasonably expect to succeed in a plot to kill him.

In conclusion, while literally the term parricide is very limited and circumscribed, it has acquired quite a rich and varied sphere of signification in Western historical and political terminology, rooted as both are in classical culture. While, for example, the *Random House Dictionary* defines parricide as the "person who commits the act of killing one's father, mother, or other close relative," the Humanist tradition, faithful to the synonymity of "father" with "ruler," extends the meaning of the word to the killer of the prince. The frequency with which the killing of the ruler, starting with Greek tragedy, is carried out by a member of the ruler's family, helped support the integration at the symbolic level. Thus, in our culture, the killer of the ruler and the parricide are two closely associated archetypes.

The second relevant aspect of Brutus' character that has influenced his interpretation is his intellectualism, which alone greatly contributed to the making of his legend. By definition intellectual pursuits are difficult to harmonize with the world of action. The mind is more inclined toward doubts than simple and fast resolutions, while action follows decision, which is synonymous with choice and option. When different choices are available, the intellectual may ponder over the merit of each and never come to a definitive solution, while the person of action—in order to make action possible—must opt for one of the choices, automatically discarding all the others. The word *decision* is supposedly derived from the Latin *de* and *caedere*, meaning "to cut off from," a verb originally used to describe the act of killing a criminal by cutting off, or severing, his head. Once that decision has been taken and the "head severed," there is no possibility of correction. Unlike intellectual discourse, action's consequences are usually permanent.

The story of Brutus, like the story of many of his followers such as Lorenzino de' Medici and Hamlet, exposes the drama of the intellectual who realizes the necessity of action. This realization is a highly dramatic element that adds suspense and breadth to the development of the Brutus story, especially in drama. Plutarch recalls how Caesar, upon hearing Brutus speak in public for the first time, exclaimed: "I know not what this young man wants, but all that he wants he wants it very much."[8] Caesar's comment is significant as it describes all the doubts that typically haunt the inquiring mind. It also shows what difficulties the mind encounters in its attempt to reach the absolute truths for which it strives and to which it would like to dedicate all its attention. Bringing Caesar's comment to more direct fruition and giving it the dramatic meaning of an omen of an impending tragedy, Shakespeare thus lets Brutus describe himself to Cassius in their famous dialogue of act 1 of *Julius Caesar:*

> Vexed I am
> Of late with passions of some difference,
> Conceptions only proper to myself,
> Which give some soil, perhaps, to my behaviours;
> But let not therefore my good friends be griev'd
> (Among which number, Cassius, be you one)
> Nor construe any further my neglect,
> Than that poor Brutus, with himself at war,
> Forgets the shows of love to other men.[9]

If Brutus is a tragic hero, his flaw may also be explained in part by the contradictions of thought and action inside of him. As he is described in discussing the moralities of the political situation that is forming—and in which he is an actor—as he does in Lucan's *Pharsalia*, his prestige is untouched and the nobility of his soul uncontaminated. But when he takes part in the intrigues of politics and decides not to participate in, but to guide the conspiracy against Caesar, he disgraces his intellectual and moral persona. Brutus, not Caesar, has been called the tragic hero of Shakespeare's *Julius Caesar* and of other plays on the same subject. If this is true, Brutus' intellectualism and the questions and problems of turning intellectual meditation into definite resolutions and actions may well be the centerpieces of his tragic failure. While Brutus' hesitations and dilemmas add drama to the event and allow the tragic plot to portray the hero as torn between crucial antinomies, the resolution of the dilemmas through the decision to act set in motion the tragic destiny that will bring the hero to his destruction.

The third aspect of the Brutus archetype is the ultimate futility of his act. One of the most crucial moments of Western history and the one most frequently represented in drama may revolve around a futile act that had no real historical consequence. By killing Caesar, Brutus accomplished exactly the same as Florentine historian Francesco Guicciardini said Lorenzino de' Medici accomplished when he killed Duke Alessandro. Like Lorenzino, whose act finally resulted in the strengthening of the Medici rule, Brutus killed a friend and a protector, made an enemy of Octavian, Caesar's successor, and ultimately justified the imperial ideal that had been his target. Also, Brutus set in motion the revenge mechanism that would lead to his own death. With this last issue, however, there is a difference: unlike Lorenzino, who was killed by Medici emissaries, Brutus took his own life when he believed that his army and that of Cassius were losing the battle at Philippi.

Questions that still remain to be answered are: What is the meaning of great, futile acts? What is their historical significance? What is their exemplary value? Why has so much interest been placed throughout the centuries on Brutus' act that failed in all its goals and, if anything, served only to confirm the new course of Roman history?

The objection can be made that Brutus did not know that his plot would not be successful and that he hoped to restore the republican system. However, the lack of preparation for what is to happen after the killing of the prince is, as Machiavelli pointed out in his chapter "On Plots" in the *Discorsi*, one of the primary reasons that many conspiracies fail.[10] It also indicates that the conspirators placed more attention on the act itself than on its consequences. The killing of the hated tyrant is just the first step in a successful plot, but a very meaningless one if it is not followed by a plan that will lead to the establishment of a new rule. It is obviously also the most noble step, the one that brings fame and glory to the killer, but it is not the one that makes the plan successful, as the case of Lorenzino de' Medici clearly shows. In the same chapter, Machiavelli goes on to describe other types of conspiracies destined to failure, and as an example, he uses the plot against Caesar. He says that killing a leader who is loved by his people is pointless. Machiavelli believes that plots against loved rulers, no matter how tyrannical, are immediately avenged by the people. And in the case of Caesar, the Roman people made sure that all the participants in the plot "would be killed in different places and at different times."[11]

The idea that some of the great moments of history may revolve around futile actions is a very seductive one. It confers existential—if not practical—meaning to human action and lends itself to a number of philosophical meditations and to the possibility of great developments in fiction and drama. This idea is as seductive and as captivating as its complement, expressed in a famous passage by Pascal, that states that everything in history depends on chance. The beauty of Cleopatra, Pascal maintained, the special features of her face, changed the course of Western history.[12] Human decisions and actions, such as those of Brutus, can accomplish little if they have no chance of succeeding. Of course, the idea of futility of action lends itself with particular force to dramatic theatre and to tragedy, as it emphasizes the role of destiny. Without destiny, many believe, there can be no tragedy.

The fourth and last aspect of the Brutus archetype is his desire of fame. Plutarch tells how in preparing for the plot and in trying to convince Brutus to participate in it, Cassius reminded him of his noble lineage and of his obligation to work against the establishment of tyranny:

> Dost thou not know thyself, Brutus? Or dost thou think that thy tribunal was covered with inscriptions by weavers and hucksters, and not by the foremost and most influential citizens? From their other praetors they demand gifts and spectacles and gladiatorial combats; but from thee, as a debt thou owest to thy lineage, the abolition of tyranny; they are ready and willing to suffer anything in thy behalf, if thou showest thyself to be what they expect and demand.[13]

Brutus' obligation to participate in the plot derives from his noble and ancient lineage. He is bound to liberty by the act of Lucius Junius Brutus, who was believed to be his ancestor and who dethroned Tarquin the Proud, the last king of Rome. According to Plutarch, this argument more than any other convinced Brutus, the intellectual and one of the most respected and most honorable Romans of his times, to act. Brutus had a debt with history and, consequently, with fame. He could not refuse his help in the name of freedom and, by doing so, acquired a place of preeminent importance in the glorious history of Rome. To maintain the nobility of his lineage Brutus had to keep the family name famous, the motivation for his participation to the anti-Caesarean plot.[14]

As with the previous archetypal element of the futility of Brutus' act, the element of fame also has a notably fatalistic streak. Fame—the search for fame, the obligation to maintain the fame of a lineage to which one belongs—deprives the individual of the freedom to choose between alternatives without constrictions. The destiny that is bestowed upon a noble Roman from birth carries with it a social and political role from which that person cannot break free.

Fame, as in the case of Lorenzino de' Medici, is often sought by those who are close to the ruler. They are often members of his family who want to kill the ruler because they believe that they were unjustly deprived of power by means of obscure political and genealogical machinations. Thus, the fame that the conspirators acquire through the execution of the ruler is their favorite type of revenge, as it deprives the ruler of the prestige and the glory of being remembered as one supported and loved by all his subjects, casts a shadow on his rule, and places the executor at least on the same level as the executed in the pages of history. While probably also an invidious passion, the craving for fame by the conspirator is a great equalizer that grows proportionally with the growth of the ruler's power, and the growth inflates the desire to kill the ruler. Power has its limits in reason and its check in envy.

The Brutus Theme in French and Italian Theatre

The four aspects of the Brutus archetype that I have just identified—parricide, intellectualism, futility of the act, and the desire of fame—are by no means the only aspects of this rich persona. They seem, however, to appear with the greatest frequency in treatments of his legend, both in literary and historical writing. They are very different elements and are not always concomitant in every revival of the Brutus figure. But when these elements appear in a single work, they tend to clash against one another. This clash creates drama, and if the clash is particularly well constructed and the elements particularly well balanced and equally opposed, drama can turn into tragedy.

The first play written on the assassination of Caesar was *Julius Caesar* by the French jurist and political thinker Marc Antoine Muret. Muret was well known as a foremost interpreter and student of Tacitus' historical philosophy and for his attempt to combine the thinking of Tacitus with that of Machiavelli, which lends a nonliberal and antidemocratic direction to his work.[15] The play, which Muret wrote at the age of eighteen, seems to anticipate the future direction of his ideas as it celebrates Caesar's ascension to the skies after his death and ends with the prophecy of the punishment of the conspirators. However, Muret's *Julius Caesar* can hardly be considered a tragedy. Its five brief acts, altogether amounting to five hundred seventy Latin verses, lend themselves to individual declamations by the main characters and the chorus rather than to dramatic dialogues and exchanges. The play is reminiscent of Seneca's *Hercules Oetaeus,* in which Hercules reaches his apotheosis in the skies after a long and glorious life. Other elements in the work are based on Seneca's Stoic ideas, such as Caesar's desire to pass to another, higher existence after death, realizing that he has reached the pinnacle of power on earth. Caesar is therefore represented as fearless of his destiny as he is about to pass from the world of the mortals to that of the gods. The apologetic view of Caesar's character is only slightly limited by his arrogance and by his sense of superiority. This last factor resolves Brutus' indecisions about whether to side with Caesar or to join the conspirators. Brutus' indecisions are, however, of crucial dramatic importance as they permit a relatively deep depiction of his personality. Despite Muret's monarchical inclinations, Brutus is in fact the main character of the play. His first speech, in which he expresses his doubts on what course of action he should take—whether to side with Caesar who saved his life or to join the conspiracy to kill Caesar because he abolished Roman freedom—contains whatever tragic element the play has to offer. The speech is probably freely drawn from sections of Lucan's *Pharsalia,* and in it Brutus realizes his duty and his destiny to join the conspiracy against Caesar:

> Let barbarians love their kings. Rome, object of fear and admiration for the world, will not. Until Brutus lives Rome will not know kings, and this one is not really a king, but a dictator. When this is the reality, what good is there in using other names? And he refuses the name, and rejects the crowns that are offered to him. This is to pretend, to play. Why would he otherwise remove the tribunes from office?
>
> But he gave me my position, and once my life. However the good of my country is more important to me than such things. He who shows himself grateful to a tyrant in his own country is really ungrateful, and foolishly tries to be grateful. It is a thing to be ashamed of![16]

The chorus' speech, which comes shortly after Brutus', underlines and reinforces the hero's position and confirms that he is destined to join the conspiracy against the dictator. While Brutus is debating his course of action, his future seems already predetermined. The theme of fate is present in the play but does not lead to tragedy. In the final act, Brutus' punishment and death are only announced by Caesar's spirit speaking from the *templa coeli* (temples of the sky)[17]: "Nec ipse cecidi: umbra cecidit tantum mea" ("I did not die, only my shadow was befallen").[18] At the same time Caesar, and later, the chorus extol the higher condition of a soul freed from the prison of the body (*corporeo carcere libero*)[19] and promise the same reward to those mortals who will preserve their faith in God. The conclusion is purposely antitragic, as it sublimates the tragic element with the promise of life after death for those who deserve it. The Christian message takes precedence over the tragic one, and the events following Caesar's assassination are left to his prophecy.

The second play on the Brutus theme was also French, written by Jacques Grévin at the age of twenty in 1558. Grévin's *César* is largely modeled on Muret's play, Grévin having been Muret's student at the College de Boncourt in Paris. However, some notable differences include the introduction of Marc Antony as an additional character who, from the beginning of the play while Caesar is still alive, vows to avenge his death. The theme of destiny, a constant preoccupation in Grévin's play, is first mentioned in the introduction in which the author claims to have been inspired by the Greek tragic poets.[20] In the first speech of act 1, Caesar predicts his own death, which Marc Antony vows to avenge long before the assassination takes place. Grévin sees destiny as a force that will preserve the monarchical rule even after Caesar's death ("Whatever may happen, when Caesar will be dead, another Caesar will avenge that evil"[21]) and not as a force that pits individuals against incredible odds and destroys them. The play is more a celebration of monarchy, obviously responding to the contingent political situation of sixteenth-century France, than an attempt to revive the tragic genre. Only the essential traits of the Brutus character are portrayed, and his antityrannical speech of act 2 is largely based on the same speech in Muret's *Julius Caesar*. Grévin wants to affirm the greatness of Caesar and to praise the monarchical cause that brought the ruler to his death, an aim made quite clear from Marc Antony's last speech to his army, which is making preparations to go to war against Brutus, and the concluding statement from a soldier:

Marc Antony:
"Come on, follow me, and show your nature and your courage for Caesar, do not fear the danger for your life while you are revenging his. I want to show to this Roman people what evils ensue from the loss of such a man if it is not revenged as it should."

. . . .

The second soldier:
"That death [Caesar's] is fatal for the new inventors of Royal power."[22]

This final statement, by one of the soldiers, who function as the chorus throughout the play, turns Caesar into a martyr who died to affirm the dignity of a new idea. Caesar may not be the hero of the play, but royal power certainly is. After all, Grévin's *Caesar* has a happy ending, since what is considered throughout the play to be the ultimate good finally asserts itself as victorious. Because of this, the tragic component of this work is difficult to see. The theme of destiny, the crucial ingredient of all great tragedy, is used here to play the role of the prophet, who anticipates from the beginning the final outcome. Theatre used for political purposes, manipulated to affirm one idea or another, is just a form of disguised political propaganda and certainly does not allow room for the great tragic themes. In tragedy, which portrays individuals under extreme and unusual, albeit possible, circumstances, neither the individuals nor the ideas triumph. This highly pessimistic literary genre, while questioning the very meaning of existence, ultimately points out the futility of human action.

A complex and often misinterpreted political message comes through, without being the work's main goal, in an Italian play on the Ides of March, Orlando Pescetti's *Cesare* published in 1594.[23] The play, considered by some scholars to have had a substantial influence on Shakespeare's *Julius Caesar* and, for certain details, also on *Hamlet*,[24] was dedicated by Pescetti to Alfonso II D'Este, Duke of Ferrara. In his introduction to the work, which centers on the conspiracy against Caesar, Pescetti hints at many similarities between Caesar and the duke and contrives a complex genealogical tree involving pagan gods along with Greek and Roman heroes to prove that the duke is Caesar's descendant. While a subject's comparison of his duke to an assassinated Roman ruler may seem quite surprising and even irreverent, it falls within a typically Italian Renaissance tradition. Renaissance princes and popes frequently ennobled them-selves by constructing genealogical trees that originated with a famous figure of Roman history or mythology. The origination of Alfonso II D'Este's genealogy with Caesar was a matter of no little importance, as Caesar founded the Roman Empire and is one of the figures of Roman history who reappears most frequently among Latin writers and poets. In the cultural situation of Renaissance Italy, teeming with classical values and infatuated with classical history to the point of a quasi-maniacal obsession, there could be no greater horror than to be identified with Caesar; Pescetti's comparison, however, did not create an identification with the negative aspects of Caesar's destiny. In his dedication to the duke, while stressing, in a manner similar to that of Machiavelli, Caesar's excesses and underlining the religious differences between classical and modern times, Pescetti writes: "If he [Caesar] had been a Christian and had been satisfied in being the first of his city, without wanting to be more powerful than his city, or had been made the legitimate ruler; and if Your Highness had the opportunity that he had to prove himself in arms, could one not say that Your Highness (both seen in your corporeal shape and in your soul) was the same as Caesar?"[25]

In referring to Caesar in his dedication, Pescetti alludes to the political issue of the abuse of power, the modern version of the tragic theme of hubris, a theme to which Machiavelli dedicated much attention in his own works and considered a matter of major impor-tance in making and destroying rulers. This abuse, along with Cae-sar's arrogance and appetite for fame, marks the difference between his rule and the legitimate one of Alfonso II D'Este. Indeed, the author also points out in the dedication that if Brutus and Cassius were living under the rule of Alfonso they would consider themselves fortunate to be governed by him.[26]

Power, the abuse of it by the one who holds it and the lust for it by the envious who do not have it, is the underlying theme of Pes-cetti's play. The very knowledge of power and of the fame that power brings with it are to Pescetti the flaws of tragic heroes that cause their inevitable destruction.

In the five acts of his *Cesare* Pescetti covers the events from the preparation for the conspiracy to the death of Caesar. The death itself, in strict observance with the principle dictating dramatic unity, occurs off stage, just as in Muret's and Grévin's plays. Despite Jupi-ter's anticipation of Brutus' punishment in the prologue, Brutus is the play's main character and its hero. Nothing disparaging is said about him, and his mistakes, if any, can be attributed in part to human weakness and in part to his faith in justice. Brutus' resolve to do justice and to bring the tyrant to death is absolute and without doubt. Unlike Shakespeare's Brutus, Pescetti's is not torn by internal doubts about what to do (possibly the only major difference between the two Brutuses). His scholarly mind is not presented as one tormented by hesitations and holding few certainties, but rather as a legalistic mind, one knowing more than others what is right and what is wrong. Pescetti's Brutus will not bend rectitude in the name of political expedience. In a dialogue in act 1, the shrewd and scheming Cassius recommends to Brutus the killing not only of Caesar, but also of Marc Antony. Cassius fears that otherwise Marc Antony might try to obtain for himself absolute control of the state. But Brutus is very firm in opposing the plan, which he believes would pervert in the eyes of the people the true meaning of their act: "If we will kill others beyond the Tyrant, the populace, that always understands things wrong and wrongfully tells them, will think that we were induced to our act not by the desire to free the state, but by private hatred and the will to take revenge; and therefore that act, from which we expect to obtain eternal fame, will give us shame and eternal scorn."[27] In Pescetti's play Brutus' intellectual nature, while not evidencing doubt and hesitation, remains important as it directs Brutus toward decisions based on an abstract sense of justice, not on political expedience. The decision to save Marc Antony's life, which springs from his uncompromising posture, will in the end be the cause of his demise.

The desire for fame in Pescetti's play is an overwhelming reality. None of the major characters are immune to it and, in some cases, it thwarts their ability to reason correctly and to decide wisely. In the speech by Brutus just quoted, his decision not to kill Marc Antony derives, of course, from his sense of justice, but he had probably also considered his historical posterity. His intention to act appropriately is largely motivated by his desire to acquire eternal fame as one of the great Romans in history who always acted in the name of moral values. Not surprisingly, the first scene of the play shows Brutus in a dialogue with the ghost of Pompey, and some critics believe that the apparition may have influenced the creation of Caesar's ghost in Shakespeare's play.[28] In his meeting with Pompey, the glorious Roman who fought Caesar and with whom Brutus sided, Brutus promises to kill the tyrant, thus repeating the glorious act of his ancestor, Lucius Junius Brutus, who freed Rome from the king Tarquin the

Proud. With his act Brutus expects to enter into eternity and to be remembered in his city's annals as its savior. Cassius, also aware of Brutus' desire for a place in history, tries to strengthen his intent to participate in the plot by telling him: "This is the way, Brutus, which brings to the Skies, by killing Tyrants."[29]

The type of fame that Marc Antony seeks is quite different from that of Brutus. As he expects to become Caesar's successor, to Marc Antony fame is connected to power, as shown by his articulation of his desires even before Caesar is dead:

> Oh, if the skies could ever give me such good, if I could see myself with a golden crown around my temples and my hands holding a scepter full of gems; if I could ever see Rome, and its vassal Kings kneeling, pay homage and promise obedience to me, who would be happier and more pleased than I? . . .
> In the meantime I will try in any possible way to gain the favor of the people and to have the soldiers on my side, so that, if Caesar were to pass away by natural or violent death, I could set my foot on that same stone where the good star brought him.[30]

Pescetti characterizes Marc Antony as an untrustworthy and dangerous man whose concerns are centered only on power and on fame. Marc Antony is, deep inside, a traitor to Caesar, even if destiny wants Caesar to fall by another hand.

The most interesting representation of the fame theme in Pescetti's *Cesare* involves Caesar. Like Muret and Grévin, Pescetti describes Caesar as a man who believes himself to be closer to the gods than to other human beings. He expresses this belief in a rather theatrical scene in which Caesar responds to the praises of the untrustworthy and deceptive Marc Antony. After Marc Antony describes Caesar's actions and his person with the adjective *divino*, the Latin etymology of which means "belonging to God," Caesar replies: "With the princely praises with which you honor me, oh Anthony, I am very pleased; and rightfully so because they come from he who seeing the truth is used to say it, and who speaks what is in his heart, who is so wise and candid that as he cannot deceive himself in his judgments, and who in speaking does not want to deceive others."[31] Thus, by believing in his own greatness, Caesar commits the same mistake that he commits by trusting Marc Antony. The two are actually inseparable. Caesar has no doubt that Marc Antony is speaking the

truth because he believes that his own nature has more to share with
that of the gods than with that of humans. To use a rather striking
metaphor by Oswald Spengler, Caesar believes that as the ruler
chosen by destiny, he is identical to destiny: "And he who is to himself
a Destiny (like Napoleon) does not need this insight of symbols of
destiny, since between himself as a fact and the other facts there
is a harmony of metaphysical rhythm which gives decisions their
dreamlike certainty."[32]

Simply by substituting Pescetti's Caesar for Spengler's Napoleon
we obtain a perfect description of Caesar's portrayal in the play.
Because Caesar believes that he has been provided with a special and
superhuman condition, he thinks that for him, unlike other mortals,
destiny will follow his wishes. Indeed, in his long dialogue with his
wife Calpurnia, certainly one of the most dramatic and well-written
sections of the play, Caesar refuses to accept as "symbols of destiny"
the supernatural phenomena that Calpurnia sees as omens of her
husband's imminent death and in the name of which she tries to
dissuade him from going to the Senate:

> If these omens are indications of a danger impending over my
> life, it is necessary that what they predict will happen; otherwise
> they are false omens, and it is stupid to pay attention to them.
> But if what they predict is to happen necessarily, who can
> oppose it and stop it from happening? Who can avoid the
> inevitable? How many times does it happen that someone,
> believing that he is avoiding a danger, actually goes towards it,
> and finds his death where he thinks to be safe? Who knows that
> the danger is not there where you advise me to stay?[33]

With this statement, while raising a crucial point in the philosophical
discussion about free will, Caesar does not accept as "symbols of
destiny" the supernatural phenomena previously described by the
priest and Calpurnia and feared by them as omens of impending
tragedy. If he were observant of traditional Roman values and religion, he would not walk to the Senate because he would feel subjected, like all mortals, to the obscure forces of destiny. But Caesar,
assured of his greatness by his glorious deeds and by the flattery of
Marc Antony, thinks that he has broken the confines of traditional
Roman culture. Roman destiny does not apply to him because he has
changed it. The forces that control his life, Caesar believes, are

more powerful and more enigmatic forces than those described by Calpurnia and the priest, who, by looking at fearful natural phenomena, are unable to see mystery itself. Caesar is destiny, and the destiny of destiny is mystery—God himself.

The other two elements of the Brutus archetype, the act of parricide and its futility, are not as fully developed in Pescetti's play as the themes of Brutus' intellectualism and his desire for fame. Parricide is briefly and rather enigmatically referred to in one of Brutus' initial speeches, when in discussing the Roman state enslaved under Caesar's dictatorship, he calls it *la madre nostra* (our mother), an expression that may refer in this case both to *patria* (motherland) and to Brutus' mother, Servilia, Caesar's lover. Caesar, who is not mentioned in this speech other than by the term *tiranno* (tyrant), may function symbolically as the surrogate father figure who will be soon killed.[34]

Some speeches by both Cassius and Brutus indicate their concern that their act against Caesar will ultimately only be important as a glorious act without any lasting consequences in Roman history. However, this idea is most forcefully expressed by the chorus in the concluding speech of the play, a speech expressing a Stoic vision of human history and human activity as guided by pointless madness. In this context, not only Brutus and Cassius' act but human action as a whole becomes futile. The chorus says that humankind must learn the lesson of the repetitious and meaningless cycles of history, made of war and battles, deaths and all other evils. Individuals must learn how to confront their own final moments with vigor and abnegation:

> Open your eyes, oh blind man, and after having rid yourself from the fog of passions, with a clear and impartial vision look at the workings of nature, and with me you will see clearly that this world is a perpetual war, in which one kills the other, and as soon as one dies another one is born, and the world renews itself. So, since one must die, and against death knowledge and strength have little power, let us get ready to receive death with a strong and courageous heart. . . .[35]

The chorus' message in this concluding speech of the play is an invitation to shift attention from the world of political events and of social activity to that of the soul, which is the world that belongs exclusively to the individual. The playwright's final question seems to be: what can humankind learn from great events such as Caesar's assassination? Pescetti's Stoicism is most evident in the concluding scene when he interprets the terrible strife needed to bring down Caesar as simply paving the road for another Caesar ("as soon as one dies another one is born.") Humankind, Pescetti concludes, must learn from the tragedies of history that history is destined to be tragic and to tragically repeat itself.

It is difficult to determine whether Orlando Pescetti's *Cesare* is a tragedy in its own right or if it only expresses a tragic view of history. Definitions of this kind depend largely on the critical point of view and, especially, on the definition of tragedy itself. However, Pescetti's *Cesare*, unlike Shakespeare's *Julius Caesar*, would probably not survive very long on the stage in our modern times, an indication that the play lacks theatricality. Nevertheless, certain aspects of *Cesare* are important for our study of Brutus. Pescetti succeeded in giving the Brutus character a rich and complex dramatic treatment and in inserting in his work many of the archetypal elements that have been part of our discussion of the Roman Brutus and of the Renaissance Brutuses. In doing so Pescetti was instrumental in revitalizing the Brutus character so that it was more relevant to his times. He prepared Brutus for the great transformation that the character was to receive in Shakespeare's *Julius Caesar* and *Hamlet*. Although the Brutus archetype may be unequally treated in Pescetti and not given, in some cases, the emphasis it deserves, *Cesare* succeeds in summing up, in one work, all the points that were developed during the Renaissance revival of Brutus from Dante to Lorenzino de' Medici. The work also presented the character as a universal example of a core of interesting human traits. Unlike history and life and more so than literature, theatre, especially Renaissance theatre, tried to present human happenings with universal exemplary values. Theatre presents recognizable events and characters in which viewers can see something of themselves. That Pescetti, his predecessors Muret and Grévin, and his successor Shakespeare all decided to use Caesar and Brutus as the main characters of plays written at the threshold of the great theatrical renaissance of modern times should give us reason to meditate. Obviously both Caesar and Brutus represented an important aspect of the moral and the psychological condition of humankind at the dawn of the modern age. This aspect is vast and complex, but power, a word both very sinister and extremely captivating, may contain the secret of its explanation.

The Shakespearean Brutus

Shakespeare's *Julius Caesar*, the culminating play on tyrannicide of the Renaissance period that inspired other plays on the Ides of March written from the seventeenth century until modern times, stands as one of the greatest works of Western literature. It enjoys constant productions, infinite interpretations, and because of its wealth of moral and political ideas and problems, frequent reference and quotation. *Julius Caesar* is commonly referred to in discussing political and historical matters of power and its exercise.

Plutarch's *Lives* is considered to be if not the only by far the most important source for *Julius Caesar*, although Plutarch is not a source that can help us better understand and interpret the play. The plot and the characters of *Julius Caesar* are doubtlessly taken from Plutarch, who uses the traditional figures of the crucial and momentous events of Roman history that the play represents. However, the routine definition of *Julius Caesar* as a "Roman" play attaches to it a connotation at once restrictive and thematically incorrect. *Julius Caesar* is obviously Roman as far as its subject is concerned. The term Roman is also used to distinguish a group of Shakespearean plays. But when we are led to believe that Shakespeare's Roman plays are interpretations of Roman history, we are greatly misled. Shakespeare's *Julius Caesar* is in all its aspects and especially in its ideology a quintessentially Renaissance work with its roots firmly grounded in the Italian tradition.

In a detailed study with many line-by-line comparisons, Alexander Boecker, a Shakespearean scholar, has demonstrated beyond doubt that various sections of *Julius Caesar* were directly inspired by Orlando Pescetti's *Cesare*.[36] However, Shakespeare's debt to the Italian Renaissance goes far beyond his borrowings from Pescetti's play. In the Brutus-Caesar theme, one much discussed during the Renaissance, Shakespeare found the perfect metaphor for his analysis of power at the dawn of the modern age and at the beginning of the modern monarchical state. The principal subject of Shakespeare's *Julius Caesar*, like Machiavelli's *Prince*, is a new understanding of monarchical power and how it is justified, envied, imitated, attacked, and compromised in the presence of the its opposing force, republicanism. The Italian Renaissance city-state and the other modern European states, born of the struggle between the necessity of absolute power and the needs and ideals of democracy, reflect the conflict between expediency and the ideals of freedom that reject monarchical rule. Despite the hatred it drew and all the constitutional limitations it violated, absolute power became a necessity for the new European monarchies. The science of government had not yet reached the sophistication of modern times, when power is carefully disguised and appropriately distributed among various political bodies so that it is at once more elusive and less detestable. For the Renaissance, absolute power was monarchy, hated by many but justified by Machiavelli as necessary for the state's survival.[37]

In *Julius Caesar* Shakespeare gives us vivid depictions of power from very different points of view. Each of the main characters in the play represents one aspect of this varied reality, starting with Caesar who is power itself. In his characterization of the absolute leader, Shakespeare portrayed the blinding effects that unlimited power carries with it. It is not monarchical power in itself but its psychological effects—Caesar's detachment from others and his sense of absolute superiority—that bring Caesar to his death, as he indicates in his brief speech in the Senate just before he is stabbed:

> But I am constant as the northern star,
> Of whose true fix'd and resting quality
> There is no fellow in the firmament.
> The skies are painted with unnumbered sparks,
> They are all fire, and every one doth shine;
> But there's but one in all doth hold his place.
> So in the world: 'tis furnish'd well with men,
> And men are flesh and blood, and apprehensive;
> Yet in the number I do know but one
> That unassailable holds on his rank,
> Unshak'd of motion; and that I am he.[38]

Caesar speaks the three remaining lines of this speech and is stabbed by Cinna. Just before he is stabbed, he asks his killer: "Hence! Wilt thou lift up Olympus!" Indeed, Caesar is not a god of Olympus, and his thinking to the contrary exposes the reason for his fall. He represents power that has grown too much above human control, a power that instead of infusing security, comfort, and a sense of justice among the citizens, introduces the fear of abuses. Its prerogatives have become unlimited, its boundaries unclear.

The other aspect of power, that it is a necessity and a permanent reality as well as often the result of evil machinations, is represented by Marc Antony, the shrewd Machiavellian politician and the ultimate political survivor who manages to turn a negative situation to his advantage. The essence of Marc Antony's personality is represented in his speech, a masterpiece of deception given after the death of Caesar. Without actually condemning the conspirators' act, Marc Antony succeeds in turning popular opinion against them, thus becoming himself the inheritor of Caesar's public support. The play's significant ending with the victory of Marc Antony and Octavian—although the victory materializes because of Cassius' tragic misunderstanding concerning the progress of the battle—confirms a negative and evil view of power.

Cassius is equally Machiavellian, although not endowed with the same amount of stamina and endurance as Marc Antony. At the beginning of the play he understands the potential dangers posed by Marc Antony and proposes to Brutus that they should kill him along with Caesar. Brutus, unwilling to compromise the morality of the conspiracies and indifferent to the political necessities of the situation, firmly opposes Cassius' idea, thus allowing his future destroyer to survive. In Shakespeare's play the demise of Brutus and of Cassius is caused by two personal flaws that deprive them of the ability to acquire and maintain power. Brutus is flawed by an abstract, intellectual sense of justice that constantly clashes with political expediency and that reaches its climax in the fatal decision to save Marc Antony's life at the Ides of March. On the other side, the shrewd and Machiavellian Cassius is marred by his pessimism, or "melancholy" as Shakespeare calls it. Fearing, without reason or proof, that Brutus' army is being defeated like his own at Philippi—while it is actually winning—Cassius orders his servant Pindarus to kill him, thus setting in motion the beginning of the end for the republican side. Shakespeare's message is that the powerful cannot indulge in pessimism or human weaknesses and passions. The preservation of power requires endurance, indifference, and a firm belief in the existence of destiny.

The final clue to the understanding of *Julius Caesar* rests primarily on Shakespeare's description of Cassius and, especially, of Brutus. In act 1, as the playwright introduces the two conspirators, he seems to give them qualities derived from elements in Plutarch,[39] Sallust's description of Catiline, and Poliziano's descriptions of the Pazzi conspirators. Shakespeare also uses several physical connotations to describe Cassius that seem adopted from Sallust's descriptions of Catiline. In his portrayal of Brutus, while probably still relying on Sallust's Catiline and eliminating the negative qualities through the influence of Plutarch, Shakespeare stresses the psychological and moral aspects. In his dialogue with Marc Antony in act 1, Caesar expresses his fears of Cassius and justifies them by Cassius' unkempt looks:

> Let me have men about me that are fat,
> Sleek men, and such as sleep o' nights.
> Yond Cassius has a lean and hungry look;
> He thinks too much: such men are dangerous.[40]

Thus the classical, and possibly eternal, physical connotations of the conspirator and the covert plotter enter the play from the beginning and create an aura of suspense. But Brutus' descriptions of himself, ("Vexed I am / Of late with passions of some difference" and "Poor Brutus, with himself at war,"[41]) while also reminding us of similar descriptions by Sallust and Poliziano, add a moral and dramatic tone to the entire play. Since nothing negative is said about Brutus in all of *Julius Caesar*, his internal doubts add a psychological and a theatrical dimension to the dramatic development. If indeed *Julius Caesar* is a political play centered around the theme of power, Brutus, and Brutus alone, transforms it into a moral one. His uncertainties result from his desire to act not according to the rules of power but to the rules of his high sense of justice. This factor is, however, also the cause of Brutus' failure. Power is indifferent to justice and Brutus represents the failure of a political agenda caused by a moral and a psychological tragedy. The Stoic and intellectual Brutus, "the noblest Roman" as he is called by his enemies in the closing scene of the play,[42] the virtuous descendant of another Brutus who freed his city from monarchy, is torn throughout the first two acts of the play—until the death of Caesar—by the dilemma of action versus thought. Stoicism, the new fashionable philosophy of Rome, the new philosophy of thought and introspection that opposes the traditional philosophy of action, would incline Brutus to be detached from political matters and to retreat into the world of ideas. But he cannot, for he is a noble Roman descended from an old republican family and he must act to redress a wrong committed by Caesar to the tradition of the Roman political system. Brutus acts for justice and not for power. Power, itself a center of evils, turns around to punish him. The dilemmas expressed in the tragedy of Brutus—thought versus action, justice versus power, old values versus new ones—are typically Renaissance dilemmas, similar to the ones previously examined in the Florentine conspiracies of the fifteenth and sixteenth centuries.

Through its complex and bloody political evolution, the Italian experience of the city-state and the French and English experience of the monarchical state and its internal strifes and religious wars, the Renaissance developed a new understanding of power as both an evil and a necessity. Gone were the medieval and classical philosophies of power inspired and guided by God, and gone also was the belief that the monarch was the earthly representative of God, at least in central and northern European states. Power belonged to whoever acquired it, by whatever means, and the realities of politics show that nothing can be, or should be, done to prevent the workings of power because it is necessary for the state.

The tragedy of Brutus is the tragedy of many Renaissance tyrannicides who miserably failed in their cause. It is the tragedy of fighting both a new system in the name of traditional values and an accepted and recognized evil such as power—represented by Caesar's dictatorship—in the name of justice. The modern state has no more room for these Brutuses. Their moralistic attitude and their intransigence are seen as condescending and arrogant as well as futile. The injustices Brutus points out are obvious and universally known but Brutus is no longer needed to act as a moral arbiter.

Conclusion

The Brutus myth remained alive through modern times when it was sinisterly revived by some twentieth-century terrorist organizations. In the glorious revolutionary times of the eighteenth century and during the Italian Risorgimento, the figure of Brutus lived up to its illustrious past in the memories of many French and American antimonarchical fighters. Some important authors also composed moving and beautiful works on the Brutus legend. In 1731 Voltaire wrote the play *La Mort de César*. In 1774 Herder dedicated a famous cantata to him, *Brutus*, which was set to music by J. C. F. Bach, son of Johann Sebastian. Vittorio Alfieri, who was obsessed throughout his work by the struggle between freedom and tyranny, dedicated to Marcus Brutus his famous play *Bruto Secondo*. Finally, one of the nineteenth century's greatest poets, Giacomo Leopardi, dedicated one of his early poems, *Bruto Minore*, to the Roman hero. While a brief and selected list, it sufficiently indicates the celebrity that the killer of Caesar enjoyed in post-Renaissance European culture and history.

The ethical and political problems raised by more recent examinations of Brutus in literature and political theory are substantially different from the ones that I have discussed and would deserve a separate literary and historical analysis in their own right. My conclusion of the discussion with Shakespeare's *Julius Caesar*—along with the appendix that follows in which I attempt to justify a possible similarity between the figures of Brutus and Hamlet in Shakespeare's play—is by no means arbitrary. My intention was to describe the development of the Brutus myth from Roman and Greek to Renaissance authors. What interested me was the clash—so vividly expressed by Dante—between classical moral values and Christian ones that occurred around the Brutus figure and the attempt at a compromise between the two views made by so many Renaissance writers. The clash and the compromise that we have observed with Brutus are at once symptomatic and exemplary of the way in which the entire corpus of classical culture was transmitted to, and transformed in, the early modern European worldview. I wanted to observe Brutus caught in the struggle between free will and destiny, expediency and morality, freedom and absolute power, the real and the ideal. The need to come to terms with this struggle and to describe a new path for human morality gave birth to some of the most interesting works of early European literature.

While we have progressed immensely from the ethical problems posed by Dante and his followers, the moral and psychological struggle that attracted much of their attention is, at least in part, still present in modern times, ready both to haunt us and to make us feel more human.

Appendix
Notes
Bibliography
Index

Appendix

Hamlet as a New Brutus

In two books written almost thirty years apart, the leading English Shakespeare critic at the turn of the century, Sir Israel Gollancz, discusses the substantial similarities between the Hamlet and Brutus figures. Gollancz' studies are interesting because he compares the Hamlet story to works of northern origin and, instead of Marcus Junius Brutus, killer of Caesar, he refers to Lucius Junius Brutus of early Roman legend, the hero who freed the city from its cruel last king, Tarquin the Proud. In these two books, *Hamlet in Iceland* and *The Source of Hamlet*,[1] published in 1898 and in 1926 respectively, Gollancz points out that one probable source for the Hamlet story can be found in Snorri Sturluson's *Prose of Edda*, in which reference is made to a certain "Amlodi," but strongly suggests that Saxo Grammaticus' *Historia Danica* is the most likely source for Shakespeare's play. He adds that Saxo's story, in which Hamleth takes revenge over his uncle Feng who has murdered his father Horwendil and married his mother Gerutha, closely resembles Livy's story of Lucius Junius Brutus, who liberated Rome from the kings. In Livy's Roman history, Brutus, son of Tarquinia, the sister—and possibly also the wife[2]—of Tarquin the Proud, who had usurped the reign of Servius Tullius, drives the king from Rome. In commenting on the similarities between Saxo and Livy, Gollancz says:

> It is clear from this, that however much the Hamlet story may have already resembled the Brutus story before its appearance in Danish History, Saxo must have recognized the kinship of the two stories, and added to their common traits. These points

of contact, however, belong only to the earlier career of Hamlet, as narrated in Saxo's Third Book. An ingenious theorist has even gone so far as to maintain that the Hamlet story is nothing more than a Northern transformation of the Roman Brutus saga.[3]

Lucius Junius Brutus of early Roman legend is obviously not Marcus Junius Brutus, although it is not difficult to find in the Hamlet figure a combination of the two Roman Brutuses. This combination is, in fact, already present in Roman historiography, in which Marcus Junius Brutus is often called the descendant of Lucius Junius Brutus and especially the inheritor of his role as a liberator. As a reader of Plutarch and a student of Roman history, Shakespeare, who had developed the Brutus character in *Julius Caesar*, was well aware of the traditional assimilation of the two Brutuses.

However, another etymological and behavioral element makes the assimilation even more compelling. Gollancz hypothesizes that "the name 'Amlodi,' from which Hamlet is derived, was merely a translation of the Latin 'Brutus,' i.e. 'The Dullard.'"[4] Following Gollancz, Giorgio de Santilliana writes in *Hamlet's Mill*: "The name *Amleth*, *Amlodhi*, Middle English *Amlaghe*, Irish *Amlaidhe*, stands always for 'simpleton,' 'stupid,' 'like unto a dumb animal.' It also remained in use as an adjective. Similarly, as an adjective, *brutus* in Latin means "passive," "neutral," "procrastinating," "unable to make up one's mind," and, finally, "stupid."[5] Interestingly the Latin language combines in the same word the two concepts of stupidity and indecision. In fact, Livy tells us that to survive at Tarquin's court and escape his legendary cruelty, Lucius Junius Brutus purposely tried to be considered stupid (*ex industria factus ad imitationem stultitiae*)[6] and happily agreed to be called Brutus, a name that confirmed his supposed mental condition. In Plutarch's life of Marcus Junius Brutus, the other connotation of the adjective that relates not to stupidity but to indecision haunts the future killer of Caesar. He is described as "immersed in calculation and beset with perplexities,"[7] while Caesar is reported to have exclaimed this famous pronouncement about him: "I know not what this young man wants, but all that he wants he wants it very much."[8]

Shakespeare, in producing *Hamlet*, possibly created a literary patchwork, that is, his character of Hamlet, while preserving some traits of the older Hamlet who is linked to the connotations of the word *Amlodi,* exhibits personality aspects from both Brutuses. In this interpretation, Shakespeare's Hamlet unites in his personality and character the pretended stupidity of Lucius Junius Brutus and the philosophical indecisions and perplexities of Marcus Junius Brutus. By doing so Shakespeare created a new type of personality, one not known previously in Western literature. While the man of wisdom who pretends to be stupid (*stulti sapiens imitator*) is a very old and common character, as is the intellectual who is unable to make up his mind when action is required, the combination of real or pretended stupidity with philosophical perplexity is both unique and psychologically intriguing.

In Shakespeare's play, the young, learned, and idealistic Hamlet is confronted with a reality—his uncle's marriage to his mother after the killing of his father—that he would prefer not to acknowledge. This reality, hidden in the collective subconscious of the political system of his and all times, is not usually encountered in political scenarios described in books. To escape this reality, Hamlet withdraws to reading and philosophical meditation. Unlike Sophocles' Oedipus, who hastens to confirm his suspicions as soon as he suspects that a terrible crime was committed, Hamlet tries to repress the idea. While the classical Greek hero believes that evil crimes can be punished and their consequences redressed, the modern hero, represented by Hamlet in the famous "To be, or not to be" speech, wonders whether it is better to stoically endure the evils of fortune or to act against them:

> To be or not to be: that is the question:
> Whether 'tis nobler in the mind to suffer
> The slings and arrows of outrageous fortune,
> Or to take arms against a sea of troubles,
> And by opposing, end them.[9]

While Oedipus, a prototype for the classical hero, has no doubts and thinks that political order can be restored, Hamlet is torn between an ideal and a real view of the political world. He is divided between a bookish, classical view of human affairs and a modern, real one and expresses this division in his response to Polonius, the prototype of rhetorical and classical learning, when Polonius asks him about the object of his reading. "Words, words, words,"[10] Hamlet answers, indicating his loss of faith in the empty and sterile legacy of the written text.

Like the Italian Renaissance writers in their political treatises and historical commentaries that culminated in the work of Machiavelli, Shakespeare in his political plays gives us a view of power as a necessary evil. The young Hamlet's loss of innocence and unwillingness to acknowledge reality can function as a metaphor for Western culture's revolution in political theory and practice during the Renaissance. Hamlet's initial disbelief in the realities of the situation and his ensuing awkward behavior are indeed interpreted by Polonius and others at court as madness. The only exception is the usurping king himself, who considers Hamlet's unusual behavior as a dangerous form of melancholia[11] and decides to have him killed, but the murder attempt proves unsuccessful. In the tragic ending of the play both the guilty and the innocent die, a clear message from Shakespeare regarding justice in the political world. The same ending is not contemplated in the work of Saxo Grammaticus, the playwright's principal source.

At the conclusion of the Renaissance, between the end of the sixteenth century and the beginning of the seventeenth century when Shakespeare wrote his plays, England and other European states were forced by political necessity to erect strong, centralized monarchies. The European political situation, characterized by countries competing for territory and, shortly thereafter, colonial dominance, required rulers to be in total control of their kingdoms. The concept of *ragion di stato* (reason of state) took precedence over justice and morality. The overwhelming influence of Machiavelli's writings, especially *The Prince*, adds fuel to the intellectual justification of this political reality. Perhaps Shakespeare designed his *Hamlet* to portray, if not to justify, the reality of absolute power as a necessity that transcends justice and morality.

After having examined the classical tyrannicidal archetype in *Julius Caesar*, in which the figure of Brutus, despite his final failure, is presented with the nobility of a Greek hero and with the Stoic intellect of a Roman philosopher, Shakespeare confronted the modern killer of the king in *Hamlet*. Hamlet's youthful innocence and unwillingness to believe the obvious might be contrasted with the lost innocence of Western civilization that once justified royal power only by virtue of tradition and of religious principles. The king that Hamlet decides to kill is indeed a usurping king, a king who has committed a terrible crime, but he is nevertheless a king who holds power. Hamlet's refusal to understand that power is indifferent to good and evil is the cause of his demise. Unlike *Oedipus Rex*, *Hamlet* is not a tragedy of the morality of politics but a tragedy of its reality.

I have tried to show through evidence derived from textual analysis and based on thematic motives that the Hamlet figure is an evolution and transformation of the Brutus archetype that had developed during the Renaissance and culminated in Shakespeare's own *Julius Caesar*. In concluding, I must add that the evolution and the transformation are significant. Hamlet's madness, whether pretended or real, and his mind-splitting hesitations and doubts deprive him of the heroic nobility that is still present in Brutus. Hamlet's youth, his childish attitudes towards his mother and Ophelia, and his often aimless hesitations all make him a character who is probably able to kill an evil tyrant, but certainly not one who can, in turn, hold power. In characterizing Hamlet by showing his many weaknesses and shortcomings, Shakespeare probably wanted to remove the tyrannicidal figure from the mainstream of modern political thinking. Neither a philosopher nor a politician—perhaps just a dilettante in both of these fields—Shakespeare's Hamlet resembles a romantic anti-hero more than a classical hero. Like a Russian nihilist of the past century or a modern terrorist, Shakespeare's Hamlet inhabits the fringes of political life and society. He is unable to find a role for himself. His ambitions are bigger than his abilities; his striving for the ultimate, decisive act is simply visionary. Dreaming of an ideal past that exists no longer and unable to understand the meaning and the role of power in the modern European state, Hamlet's dreams end in a tragedy of errors that leaves no winners. With Hamlet's death dies a great hero and a great archetype of our cultural past. The noble Brutus, the hero of tradition portrayed by most classical historians and later revived in a slightly different form in the literature and the life of the Renaissance, dies forever with the indecisive and weak Hamlet. Brutus' main enemies are Machiavelli and the modern state, in which power takes precedence over morality. After Hamlet, or beginning with him, the tyrannicidal archetype survives through modern times as a misunderstood and enigmatic character who lives in hiding and dreams of impossible worlds, incapable of understanding the workings of the modern state and unable to contribute to its evolution.

The institutionalization of the political system and process decreases direct political participation. In modern society the responsibility of upholding justice and redressing an evil no longer belongs to the individual, as was the case with Brutus and was generally so in his classical world. As power becomes more institutionalized, more elusive, and especially more universally accepted as a necessary evil, the Brutus archetype, transformed into a Hamlet, survives as a figure living in the shadows, capable only of regaining full force when institutions experience a crisis or a breakdown.

Notes

1. The Making of a Destiny

1. Dante refers to Virgil in *Inferno* 1.85, as his "master" and "author": "Tu se' lo mio maestro e 'l mio autore" ("Thou art my master, and my author thou") (trans. D. L. Sayers [New York: Penguin Books, 1984]). Any further notes concerning *The Divine Comedy* refer to this translation.

2. Dante, *Inferno* 34.54–69.

3. Dante, *De Monarchia*, ed. L. Bertolet (Florence: Olschki, 1920), 1.10. In the notes, where no translator is indicated, the translation has been done by the author.

4. Dante, *De Monarchia* 11.1–2.

5. Horace, *Epistole*, ed. M. Ramous (Milan: Garzanti, 1985), 1.2.17–22.

6. Dante, *Il Convivio*, ed. F. Mazzoni (Turin: Tallone, 1965), 4.6.10.

7. Lucan, *Pharsalia*, trans. J. D. Duff (Cambridge: Harvard Univ. Press, 1969), 1.457–58.

8. Lucan, *Pharsalia* 2.242–85.

9. Lucan, *Pharsalia* 2.286–323.

10. Lucan, *Pharsalia* 7.586–96.

11. Seneca, "De constantia sapientis," in *Dialogorum Libri*, ed. E. Hermes (Lipsiae: In Aedibus Teubneri, 1923), 2.

12. Lucretius, *De rerum natura*, trans. W. H. D. Rouse (Cambridge: Harvard Univ. Press, 1966), 3.94–230.

13. Seneca, *De beneficiis*, ed. C. Hosius (Lipsiae: In Aedibus Teubneri, 1900), 2.20.

14. Cicero, *De Finibus Bonorum et malorum*, trans. H. Rackam (Cambridge: Harvard Univ. Press, 1967), 4.11.26–27.

15. Cicero, *De Officiis*, trans. W. Miller (Cambridge: Harvard Univ. Press, 1968), 3.4.19.

16. Cicero, *De Finibus* 3.18.60.

17. Augustine, *The City of God*,trans. G. E. McCracken, 7 vols. (Cambridge: Harvard Univ. Press, 1981), 1.22.
18. Plutarch, *Cato the Younger,* vol. 8 of *Lives,* trans. B. Perrin (Cambridge: Harvard Univ. Press, 1969), 236–411.
19. Augustine, *City of God* 1.23.
20. John of Salisbury, *Polycraticus* (Oxford: Clarendon Press, 1909), 8.17.
21. John of Salisbury, *Polycraticus* 8.19.
22. Thomas Aquinas, *De Regimine Principum* in *Opera Omnia* (Rome: de Propaganda Fide, 1882–1982), 1.6.
23. Thomas Aquinas, *Principum* 4.1.
24. "And why do we talk of these other philosophers mentioned in the preceding paragraph, when there are those who, following this line of thinking, did not care about their lives, such as Zeno, Socrates, Seneca, and many others?" (Dante, *Convivio* 3.14.8).
25. Dante, *Inferno* 13.56, 61.
26. Dante, *Inferno* 13.70–72.
27. Dante, *Purgatorio* 1.52–55.
28. Dante, *Monarchia* 3.15.16–18.
29. Cicero, *Lettere al Fratello Quinto e a M. G. Bruto,* ed. C. Vitali (Bologna: Zanichelli, 1974), 212–222.
30. Dante, *Paradiso* 17.46–69.

2. Brutus Carries Out His Destiny

1. Dante, *Monarchia* 1.11.1-3; *Purgatorio* 22.70–72.
2. See Ferruccio Martini, *Lorenzino de' Medici e il tirannicidio nel Rinascimento* (Rome: Multigrafica, 1972).
3. Donato Giannotti, *Dialogi di Donato Giannotti de' giorni che Dante consumo' nel cercare l'Inferno e 'l Purgatorio,* ed. Dioclecio Redig de Campos (Florence: Sansoni, 1939).
4. See Giorgio Barberi Squarotti, *La forma tragica del Principe e altri saggi sul Machiavelli* (Florence: Olschki, 1966).
5. Petrarch, "Al Magnifico Signore di Padova Francesco da Carrara. Come debba essere chi governa lo stato," in *Senilium Libri Epistole,* ed. U. Dotti (Turin: Utet, 1978), 760–843.
6. Petrarch, "Francesco da Carrara" 760–62.
7. Hans Baron, *The Crisis of the Early Italian Renaissance* (Princeton: Princeton Univ. Press, 1966), 152. See also 55–57.
8. Petrarch, "Francesco da Carrara" 774.
9. Petrarch, "Francesco da Carrara" 774–76.
10. Petrarch, "Francesco da Carrara" 776.
11. Petrarch, "Francesco da Carrara" 776.
12. Petrarch, "Francesco da Carrara" 776.

13. Giovanni Boccaccio, *De casibus virorum illustrium*, vol. 9 of *Tutte le opere*, ed. Vittore Branca (Milan: Mondadori, 1983), 8.

14. Boccaccio, *De casibus* 532.

15. Boccaccio, *De casibus* 542.

16. Boccaccio, *De casibus* 118.

17. Boccaccio, *De casibus* 130–32.

18. Barbara Tuchman, *The March of Folly: From Troy to Vietnam* (New York: Knopf, 1984).

19. Dante, *Paradiso*, 17.37–45.

20. Coluccio Salutati, *De fato et fortuna*, ed. C. Bianca (Florence: Olschki, 1985), 61–62.

21. Coluccio Salutati, *Tractatus de Tyranno*, ed. F. Ercole (Berlin: Rothschild, 1914), 41.

22. Salutati, *Tyranno* 43.

23. Salutati, *Tyranno* 45.

24. Salutati, *Tyranno* 53.

25. Suetonius, "Divus Julius," in *De Vita Caesarum*, trans. J. C. Rolfe, 2 vols. (Cambridge: Harvard Univ. Press, 1970), 1.82.3.

26. See Nancy S. Struever, *The Language of History in the Renaissance: Rhetoric and Historical Consciousness in Florentine Humanism* (Princeton: Princeton Univ. Press, 1970), 57–60.

27. For a complete discussion of the dates of composition of Bruni's *Dialogus*, see Hans Baron, *The Crisis of the Early Italian Renaissance* (Princeton: Princeton Univ. Press, 1966), 232–44.

28. Leonardo Bruni, "Ad Petrum Paulum Histrum Dialogus," vol. 1 of *Prosatori Latini del Quattrocento*, ed. Eugenio Garin (Turin: Einuadi, 1976), 68–70.

29. Plutarch, *Life of Brutus*.

30. Bruni, *Dialogus* 82.

31. This is a minor point. Niccoli had also criticized Dante for representing Cato as an old man, when in fact he died fairly young.

32. Bruni, *Dialogus* 88–90.

33. Cristoforo Landino, "Commento sopra la Commedia, Inferno XXXIV," in *Dante con l'espositioni di Cristoforo Landino et d'Alessandro Vellutello* (Venice: Giovanbattista Marchio' Sessa, 1578).

34. Jacob Burckhardt, *The Civilization of the Renaissance in Italy*, trans. S. G. C. Middlemore (New York: Modern Library, 1954), 273.

35. For a history of the word *modern* see Matei Calinescu, *Five Faces of Modernity: Modernism, Avant-Garde, Decadence, Kitsch, Postmodernism* (Durham: Duke Univ. Press, 1987), 13–26.

36. Burckhardt, *Civilization* 47.

37. Angelo Poliziano, *Coniurationis Commentarium*, ed. A. Perosa (Padua: Antenore, 1958); Alamanno Rinuccini, *De Libertate*, ed. E. Grassi (Santiago: Losada, 1952).

38. Luca della Robbia, "Narrazione del caso di Pietro Paolo Boscoli e di

Agostino Capponi," in vol. 1 of *Archivio Storico Italiano* (Florence: Archivio Storico Italiano, 1842), 283–309. The *Narrazione* is preceded by an essay on Luca della Robbia by F. Polidori.

39.   Lorenzino de' Medici, "Apologia," in Marcello Vannucci, *Lorenzaccio: Lorenzino de' Medici: un ribelle in famiglia* (Rome: Newton Compton, 1984), 235–44; Donato Giannotti, *Dialogi*.

40.   Plutarch, *Brutus* 4.6.

41.   Plutarch, *Brutus* 13.2.

42.   Suetonius, "Divus Julius," 82.2.

43.   Plutarch, *Brutus* 6.7.

44.   Ferruccio Martini, *Lorenzino de' Medici e il tirannicidio nel Rinascimento* (Rome: Multigrafica, 1972), 57.

45.   Franklin L. Ford, *Political Murder: From Tyrannicide to Terrorism* (Cambridge: Harvard Univ. Press, 1985), 136.

46.   Poliziano, *Coniurationis* 6.

47.   Poliziano, *Coniurationis* 7–8.

48.   Poliziano, *Coniurationis* 10.

49.   Poliziano, *Coniurationis* 11.

50.   Poliziano, *Coniurationis* 15.

51.   Poliziano, *Coniurationis* 16.

52.   Poliziano, *Coniurationis* 17.

53.   Niccolo' Machiavelli, *Discorso o Dialogo intorno alla nostra lingua*, ed. B. T. Sozzi (Turin: Einaudi, 1976), 10.

54.   Niccolo' Machiavelli, *Discorsi sopra la prima deca di Tito Livio*, in *Il Principe e Discorsi*. ed. S. Bertelli (Milan: Feltrinelli, 1973), 1.10.

55.   Machiavelli, *Discorsi* 3.6.

56.   Machiavelli, *Discorsi* 3.6.

57.   Machiavelli, *Discorsi* 3.6.

58.   Rinuccini, *Libertate* 142–44.

59.   Niccolo' Machiavelli, *Istorie fiorentine*, ed. A. Montevecchi (Turin: Utet, 1986), 8.34.

60.   Della Robbia, "Narrazione" 283–309.

61.   Della Robbia, "Narrazione" 289–90.

62.   Ford, *Political Murder* 138.

63.   Della Robbia, "Narrazione" 298.

64.   Della Robbia, "Narrazione" 301.

65.   Carmelo Bene, *Lorenzaccio* (Florence: Nostra Signora Editrice, 1986), 42–43.

66.   Benedetto Varchi, *Storia Fiorentina* (Milan: Società tipografica de' classci Italiani, 1803–4), 15.

67.   Adolfo Borgognoni, "Lorenzino di Pier Francesco de' Medici," in *Studi di letteratura storica* (Bologna: Zanichelli, 1891), 19–20.

68.   Machiavelli, *Discorsi* 3.4.

69.   Benvenuto Cellini, *Vita* (Milan:Rizzoli, 1985), 1.81.

70. Giorgio Vasari, *Bastiano detto Aristotile da San Gallo*, in *Opere*, ed.
G. Milanesi, 9 vols. (Florence: Sansoni, 1975).
71. de' Medici, "Apologia" 237.
72. de' Medici, "Apologia" 238.
73. de' Medici, "Apologia" 239.
74. de' Medici, "Apologia" 240.
75. de' Medici, "Apologia" 243–44.
76. Francesco Puccinotti, a nineteenth-century doctor, author of a study on homicidal manias.
77. Borgognoni, "Lorenzino" 101–2.
78. Edited by D. Redig de Campos (Florence: Sansoni, 1939).
79. Giannotti, *Dialogi* 88.
80. Giannotti, *Dialogi* 89.
81. Giannotti, *Dialogi* 95.
82. Giannotti, *Dialogi* 96–97.
83. Giuseppe Toffanin, *Machiavelli e il "Tacitismo"* (Naples: Guida, 1972).
84. Francisco de Quevedo, "Marco Bruto (1631 y 1644)," in *Prosa y verso*, ed. J. L. Borges and A. Bioy Casares (Buenos Aires: Emece Editores, 1948), 442.

3. Brutus, Destiny, and Tragedy

1. Plutarch, *Brutus* 5.2.
2. Suetonius, "Divus Julius" 1.82.2.
3. Eli Sagan, *At the Dawn of Tyranny: The Origins of Individualism, Political Oppression, and the State* (New York: Knopf, 1985).
4. Tacitus, *Cornelii Taciti Annalium Libri*, ed. C. D. Fisher (Oxford: Clarendon Press, 1966), 1.10.3.
5. Ronald Syme, *The Roman Revolution* (Oxford: Oxford Univ. Press, 1966), 112.
6. Aristotle, *Politics*, trans. H. Rackham (Cambridge: Harvard Univ. Press, 1977), 1311a–1312b.
7. Machiavelli, *Discorsi* 3.6.
8. Plutarch, *Brutus* 6.5.7.
9. *Julius Caesar*, in *Complete Works*, ed. W. J. Craig (Oxford: Oxford Univ. Press, 1978), act 1, sc. 2.
10. Machiavelli, *Discorsi* 3.6.
11. Machiavelli, *Discorsi* 3.6.
12. Blaise Pascal, *Pensées*, ed. L. Lafuma (Paris: Seuil, 1962), 102.
13. Plutarch, *Brutus* 6.10.6.
14. Leo Braudy, *The Frenzy of Renown: Fame and Its History* (Oxford: Oxford Univ. Press, 1986), 59.

15.   Toffanin, *Machiavelli* 140–43.

16.   Marc Antoine Muret, *Julius Caesar,* in *César de Jacques Grévin, edition critique avec une introduction et des notes,* ed. Jeffrey Foster (Paris: Nizet, 1974), act 2, lines 130–42.

17.   Muret, *Caesar* act 5, line 538.

18.   Muret, *Caesar* act 5, line 534.

19.   Muret, *Caesar* act 5, line 559.

20.   Jacques Grévin, *César,* ed. E. S. Ginsberg (Geneva: Librairie Droz, 1971), 90.

21.   Grévin, *César* act 1, lines 205–6.

22.   Grévin, *César* act 5, lines 1090–96, 1103–4.

23.   Orlando Pescetti, *Il Cesare, Tragedia* (Verona: Girolamo Discepolo, 1594).

24.   Alexander Boecker, *A Probable Italian Source of Shakespeare's "Julius Caesar"* (New York: AMS Press, 1971).

25.   Pescetti, *Cesare* "Dedication."

26.   Pescetti, *Cesare* "Dedication."

27.   Pescetti, *Cesare* act 1.

28.   Boecker, *Shakespeare's "Julius Caesar"* 28.

29.   Pescetti, *Cesare* act 1.

30.   Pescetti, *Cesare* act 3.

31.   Pescetti, *Cesare* act 3.

32.   Oswald Spengler, vol. 1 of *The Decline of the West,* trans. C. F. Atkinson (New York: Knopf, 1986), 142.

33.   Pescetti, *Cesare* act 3.

34.   Pescetti, *Cesare* act 1.

35.   Pescetti, *Cesare* act 5.

36.   Alexander Boecker, *Shakespeare's "Julius Caesar."*

37.   An excellent study of Shakespeare as an analyst of power is Stephen Greenblatt, *Shakespearean Negotiations* (Berkeley: Univ. of California Press, 1988).

38.   Shakespeare, *Julius Caesar* act 3, sc. 1, lines 60–70.

39.   In fact, some of Plutarch's characterization of Brutus may well be derived from Sallust's portrayal of Catiline.

40.   Shakespeare, *Julius Caesar* act 1, sc. 2, lines 191–94.

41.   Shakespeare, *Julius Caesar* act 1, sc. 2, lines 39–40 and 46.

42.   Shakespeare, *Julius Caesar* act 5, sc. 5.

Appendix: Hamlet as a New Brutus

1.   Israel Gollancz, *Hamlet in Iceland* (London: David Nutt, 1898) and *The Sources of Hamlet* (London: Frank Cass, 1967).

2.   Gollancz, *Hamlet in Iceland* 34; *Sources of Hamlet* 31.

3.   Gollancz, *Hamlet in Iceland* 34.

4.   Gollancz, *Hamlet in Iceland* 34–35.

5.   Giorgio de Santilliana and Hertha von Dechend, *Hamlet's Mill: An Essay on Myth and the Frame of Time* (Boston: Godine, 1977), 20.

6.   Livy, *Ab Urbe Condita*, ed. R. S. Conway and C. F. Walters, 2 vols. (Oxford: Clarendon Press, 1969).

7.   Plutarch, *Brutus* 13.2.

8.   Plutarch, *Brutus* 13.2.

9.   William Shakespeare, *Hamlet*, in *Complete Works*, ed. W. J. Craig (Oxford: Oxford Univ. Press, 1978), act 3, sc. 1, lines 56–59.

10.   Shakespeare, *Hamlet* act 2, sc. 2, line 196.

11.   There's something in his soul
O'er which his melancholy sits on brood;
And I do doubt the hatch and the disclose
Will be some danger.

Shakespeare, *Hamlet* act 3, sc. 1, lines 173–76.

Bibliography

Aquinas, Thomas. *Opera Omnia*. Rome: de Propaganda Fide, 1882–1982.

Aristotle. *Politics*. Translated by H. Rackham. Cambridge: Harvard Univ. Press, 1977.

Augustine. *The City of God*. Translated by G. E. McCracken. 7 vols. Cambridge: Harvard Univ. Press, 1981.

Barberi Squarotti, Giorgio. *La forma tragica del Principe e altri saggi sul Machiavelli*. Florence: Olschki, 1966.

Baron, Hans. *The Crisis of the Early Italian Renaissance*. Princeton: Princeton Univ. Press, 1966.

———. *Humanistic and Political Literature in Florence and Venice at the Beginning of the Quattrocento*. Cambridge: Harvard Univ. Press, 1955.

———. *From Petrarch to Leonardo Bruni: Studies in Humanist and Political Literature*. Chicago: Chicago Univ. Press, 1968.

Bene, Carmelo. *Lorenzaccio*. Florence: Nostra Signora Editrice, 1986.

Boccaccio, Giovanni. *Tutte le opere*. Edited by V. Branca. Milan: Mondadori, 1983.

Boecker, Alexander. *A Probable Italian Source of Shakespeare's "Julius Caesar."* New York: AMS Press, 1971.

Boissier, Gaston. *Cicero and His Friends*. Translated by A. D. Jones. New York: Putnam, 1922.

Borgognoni, Adolfo. "Lorenzino di Pier Francesco de' Medici." In *Studi di letteratura storica*, 19–20. Bologna: Zanichelli, 1891.

Botero, Giovanni. *Della Ragion di Stato*. Edited by C. Morandi. Bologna: Cappelli, 1930.

Braudy, Leo. *The Frenzy of Renown: Fame and Its History*. Oxford: Oxford Univ. Press, 1986.

Bruni, Leonardo. *Ad Petrum Paulum Histrum Dialogus*. Vol. 1, *Prosatori Latini del Quattrocento*. Edited by Eugenio Garin. Turin: Einuadi, 1976.

Burckhardt, Jacob. *The Civilization of the Renaissance in Italy*. Translated by S. G. C. Middlemore. New York: Modern Library, 1954.

Calinescu, Matei. *Five Faces of Modernity: Modernism, Avant-Garde, Decadence, Kitsch, Postmodernism*. Durham: Duke Univ. Press, 1987.

Cellini, Benvenuto. *Vita*. Edited by E. Camesasca. Milan: Rizzoli, 1985.

Cicero. *Cicerone, Lettere al fratello Quinto e a M. G. Bruto*. Edited by C. Vitali. Bologna: Zanichelli, 1974.

——. *De Finibus Bonorum et malorum*. Translated by H. Rackam. Cambridge: Harvard Univ. Press, 1967.

——. *De Officiis*. Translated by W. Miller. Cambridge: Harvard Univ. Press, 1968.

Clarke, Martin L. *The Noblest Roman: Marcus Brutus and His Reputation*. London: Thames, 1981.

Cochrane, Eric. *Historians and Historiography in the Italian Renaissance*. Chicago: Univ. of Chicago Press, 1981.

Dante. *Il Convivio*. Edited by F. Mazzoni. Turin: Tallone, 1965.

——. *De Monarchia*. Edited by L. Bertolet. Florence: Olschki, 1920.

——. *The Divine Comedy*. Translated by D. L. Sayers. New York: Penguin Books, 1984.

Della Robbia, Luca. "Narrazione del caso di Pietro Paolo Boscoli e di Agostino Capponi." In Vol. 1 of *Archivio Storico Italiano*, 283–309. Florence: Archivio Storico Italiano, 1842.

Ford, Franklin L. *Political Murder: From Tyrannicide to Terrorism*. Cambridge: Harvard Univ. Press, 1985.

Garin, Eugenio. *La cultura del Rinascimento: profilo storico*. Bari: Laterza, 1973.

——. *L'età nuova: Ricerche di storia della cultura dal XII al XVI secolo*. Naples: Morano, 1969.

——. *Italian Humanism: Philosophy and Civic Life in the Renaissance*. Translated by Peter Munz. New York: Harper and Row, 1965.

Giannotti, Donato. *Dialogi di Donato Giannotti de' giorni che Dante consumo' nel cercare l'Inferno e 'l Purgatorio*. Edited by Dioclecio Redig de Campos. Florence: Sansoni, 1939.

Gilbert, Felix. *Machiavelli and Guicciardini: Politics and History in Sixteenth-Century Florence*. Princeton: Princeton Univ. Press, 1965.

Gollancz, Israel. *Hamlet in Iceland*. London: David Nutt, 1898.

——. *The Sources of Hamlet*. London: Frank Cass, 1967.

Gordon, D. J. "Giannotti, Michelangelo and the Cult of Brutus." In *The Renaissance Imagination: Essays and Lectures*, edited by S. Orgel, 233–45. Berkeley: Univ. of California Press, 1975.

Greenblatt, Stephen. *Shakespearean Negotiations*. Berkeley: Univ. of California Press, 1988.

Grévin, Jacques. *César*. Edited by E. S. Ginsberg. Geneva: Libraire Droz, 1971.

Horace. *Epistole*. Edited by M. Ramous. Milan: Garzanti, 1985.

John of Salisbury. *Polycraticus*. Oxford: Clarendon Press, 1909.

Landino, Cristoforo. *Dante con l'espositioni di Cristoforo Landino et d'Alessandro Vellutello*. Venice: Giovanbattista Marchio' Sessa, 1578.

Livy. *Ab Urbe Condita*. 2 Vols. Edited by R. S. Conway and C. F. Walters. Oxford: Clarendon Press, 1969.

Lucan. *Pharsalia*. Translated by J. D. Duff. Cambridge: Harvard Univ. Press, 1969.

Lucretius. *De rerum natura*. Translated by W. H. D. Rouse. Cambridge: Harvard Univ. Press, 1966.

Machiavelli, Niccolo'. *Discorsi sopra la prima deca di Tito Livio*. In *Il Principe e Discorsi*. Edited by S. Bertelli. Milan: Feltrinelli, 1973.

———. *Discorso o Dialogo intorno alla nostra lingua*. Edited by B. T. Sozzi. Turin: Einaudi, 1976.

———. *Istorie Fiorentine*. Edited by A. Montevecchi. Turin: Utet, 1986.

Martini, Ferruccio. *Lorenzino de' Medici e il tirannicidio nel Rinascimento*. Rome: Multigrafica, 1972.

Mazzarino, Santo. *Il pensiero storico classico*. 3 Vols. Bari: Laterza, 1965–66.

de' Medici, Lorenzino. "Apologia." In *Lorenzaccio: Lorenzino de' Medici: un ribelle in famiglia*. Edited by Marcello Vannucci. Rome: Newton Compton, 1984.

Muret, Marc Antoine. *Julius Caesar*. In *César de Jacques Grévin*. Edited by Jeffrey Foster. Paris: Nizet, 1974.

Pascal, Blaise. *Pensées*. Edited by L. Lafuma. Paris: Seuil, 1962.

Pescetti, Orlando. *Il Cesare, Tragedia*. Venice: Girolamo Discepolo, 1594.

Petrarch, Francesco. *Senilium Libri, Epistole*. Edited by U. Dotti. Turin: Utet, 1978.

Plutarch. *Lives*. 11 Vols. Translated by B. Perrin. Cambridge: Harvard Univ. Press, 1969.

Pocock, John Greville Agard. *The Machiavellian Moment: Florentine Political Thought and the Atlantic Republican Tradition*. Princeton: Princeton Univ. Press, 1975.

Poliziano, Angelo. *Coniurationis Commentarium*. Edited by A. Perosa. Padua: Antenore, 1958.

de Quevedo, Francisco. "Marco Bruto (1631 y 1644)." In *Prosa y verso*. Edited by J. L. Borges and A. Bioy Casares. Buenos Aires: Emece Editores, 1948.

Radin, Max. *Marcus Brutus*. Oxford: Oxford Univ. Press, 1939.

Rinuccini, Alamanno. *De Libertate*. Edited by E. Grassi. Santiago: Losada, 1952.

Sagan, Eli. *At the Dawn of Tyranny: The Origins of Individualism, Political Oppression, and the State*. New York: Knopf, 1985.

Salutati, Coluccio. *De fato et fortuna*. Edited by C. Bianca. Florence: Olschki, 1985.

———. *Tractatus de Tyranno*. Edited by F. Ercole. Berlin: Rothschild, 1914.

de Santilliana, Giorgio, and Hertha von Dechend. *Hamlet's Mill: An Essay on Myth and the Frame of Time*. Boston: Godine, 1977.

Sasso, Gennaro. *Niccolo' Machiavelli: storia del suo pensiero politico*. Bologna: Il Mulino, 1980.

Seneca. *De beneficiis*. Edited by C. Hosius. Lipsiae: In Aedibus Teubneri, 1900.

———. *Dialogorum Libri XII*. Edited by E. Hermes. Lipsiae: In Aedibus Teubneri, 1923.

Shakespeare, William. *Complete Works*. Edited by W. J. Craig. Oxford: Oxford Univ. Press, 1978.

Spengler, Oswald. *The Decline of the West*. Translated by C. F. Atkinson. New York: Knopf, 1986.

Struever, Nancy S. *The Language of History in the Renaissance: Rhetoric and Historical Consciousness in Florentine Humanism*. Princeton: Princeton Univ. Press, 1970.

Suetonius. *De Vita Caesarum*. 2 Vols. Translated by J. C. Rolfe. Cambridge: Harvard Univ. Press, 1970.

Syme, Ronald. *The Roman Revolution*. Oxford: Oxford Univ. Press, 1966.

Tacitus. *Cornelii Taciti Annalium Libri*. Edited by C. D. Fisher. Oxford: Clarendon Press, 1966.

Toffanin, Giuseppe. *Machiavelli e il "Tacitismo."* Naples: Guida, 1972.

Tuchman, Barbara. *The March of Folly: From Troy to Vietnam*. New York: Knopf, 1984.

Vannucci, Marcello. *Lorenzaccio: Lorenzino de' Medici: un ribelle in famiglia*. Rome: Newton Compton, 1984.

Varchi, Benedetto. *Storia Fiorentina*. Milan: Società tipografica de' classci Italiani, 1803–4.

Vasari, Giorgio. *Opere*. 9 Vols. Edited by G. Milanesi. Florence: Sansoni, 1975.

Index

Accius, 42
Ad Petrum Paulum Histrum Dialogus (Bruni), 56–61, 63
Aeschylus, 121
Africa (Petrarch), 41
Alfieri, Vittorio, 115
Alitheus (*De Libertate*), 74–75
Allegory, 26–32, 60, 61
Annals, 96
Antony, Marc, 59, 103, 112–13; in Pescetti's *Cesare*, 106, 107, 108
Apologia (de' Medici), 65, 80, 85–87
Appian, 1
Aquinas, Thomas, 24, 25, 26
Aridosia (de' Medici), 85
Aristotle, 97
Atreus, 42
Augustine, 22, 23–24, 25, 26, 32
Augustus, 45, 96
Aurelius, Marcus, 1

Bach, J. C. F., 115
Bene, Carmelo, 81
Boccaccio, Giovanni, 40, 45–48, 50; in Bruni's *Dialogus*, 56, 57, 58; and Salutati, 50
Boecker, Alexander, 111

Borgognoni, Adolfo, 88
Boscoli, Pietro Paolo, 65, 76–79
Botero, Giovanni, 93
Botticelli, Sandro, 61
Bracciolini, Jacopo, 69
Bruni, Leonardo, 56–61, 62, 63, 91
Bruto Minore (Leopardi), 115
Bruto Secondo (Alfieri), 115
Brutus, Lucius Junius, 57–58, 100, 106–7, 119–20, 121
Brutus, Marcus, 1–2; as archetype, x–xi, 95–101; Boccaccio's treatment of, 46; Bruni's treatment of, 57–58, 59–60; and Cato compared, 13, 15, 17, 29, 32, 61; Dante's condemnation of, 2–5, 15, 26, 29–30, 32, 35, 51, 53; desire for fame of, 100–101, 106–7; in French theatre, 101–4; futility of act of, 99–100, 109–10; Giannotti's treatment of, 39, 65, 89–92, 93, 95; and Hamlet compared, 70, 80, 97–98, 119–24; and Horace compared, 6–7; intellectualism of, 97–98, 102, 106, 113, 114; and Junius Brutus compared, 57–58, 100,

106–7, 119–20, 121; on killing
of Caesar, 32–33; Landino on,
61–62; and Lorenzino de'
Medici compared, 80, 82, 89,
97–98, 99, 101; Machiavelli on,
71; Michelangelo's attitude
toward, ix, 38–39, 65, 81, 89–
92, 93; as model for Boscoli,
65, 76, 78; modern treatments
of, 115–16; as parricide, 18–19,
46, 50, 51, 55, 67, 96–97, 109;
Petrarch's treatment of, 44; in
the *Pharsalia*, 8–13, 98, 102;
Plutarch's biography of, 30, 37,
58, 66–67, 74, 96, 100, 130n.39;
as Renaissance fashion, 64–67;
Renaissance transformation of
story of, 36–40; Salutati's
treatment of, 51–53, 54, 55;
Seneca's view of, 17–19;
Shakespeare's treatment of, 70,
98, 111–15, 122, 123; and
Stoical influence on Dante, 15,
16, 17–19; suicide of, 26, 27–
28, 29–30, 99; Thomas
Aquinas' view of, 25; as tragic
hero, 50, 52, 98; and Ulysses
compared, 5–6
Brutus (Herder), 115
Burckhardt, Jacob, 63, 64

Cacciaguida (*Paradise*), 33–34
Caesar, Julius, ix, 23, 27; Bruni
on, 59–60; on Brutus, 98, 120;
Brutus on killing of, 32–33;
Cicero's view of, 21; Dante's
treatment of, 2, 4, 15, 26, 30–
31, 35; as father figure, 18–19,
44, 55, 67, 96, 109; fifteenth-
century Florentine attitudes
toward, 48; in French theatre,
102, 103–4; John of Salisbury
on, 24–25; Landino on, 61–62;
Machiavelli on, 70–71, 72–73;
Michelangelo on, 91–92; in

Pescetti's *Cesare*, 107–9, 110;
Petriarch's treatment of, 40–41,
42–43; in the *Pharsalia*, 8, 9–10,
11; Salutati's view of, 52, 53–
54, 60; Seneca's view of, 17–18;
Shakespeare's treatment of,
112, 114; Thomas Aquinas on,
25
Caligula, 85
Calpurnia (*Cesare*), 108, 109
Capponi, Agostino, 65, 76
da Carrara, Francesco, 40, 41
Cassius, 27, 46, 98, 99, 100; in
The Divine Comedy, 2–3, 30;
Giannotti and Michelangelo
on, 90–92; Landino on, 61–62;
in Pescetti's *Cesare*, 105, 106,
107, 109; as Renaissance
fashion, 65, 66; Salutati's
treatment of, 54, 55;
Shakespeare's treatment of,
113–14
Catiline, 67, 68, 71, 82, 113,
130n.39
Cato, 16, 17, 26, 32, 35, 127n.31;
Augustine's views on, 23–24,
32; Cicero's criticism of, 20;
and Landino's commentary on
Dante, 61; in the *Pharsalia*, 7–
10, 11–12, 13; Plutarch on, 22–
23; Seneca's view of, 14–15; as
symbol of salvation in Dante,
7–8, 15, 21–22, 27–30, 33–34
Cellini, Benvenuto, 81, 84–85, 87
Cervantes, Miguel de, 36
César (Grévin), 103–4, 105, 107,
110
Cesare (Pescetti), 104–10; fame
theme in, 106–9; and
Shakespeare's *Julius Caesar*
compared, 104, 110, 111
Charles V, Emperor, 83, 85
Charles VIII, King, 76
Christianity: attitude toward
suicide in, 22–24, 27, 30, 34;

classical world as preparation
for, 31; concept of soul in, 16;
free will in, 55; view of destiny
in, 4, 35; view of tyrannicide
in, 24–26, 76–78, 79
Cicero, 1, 19–22, 27, 31, 32–33;
Bruni on, 56–57; Petrarch on,
41, 42–44; and Salutati, 50, 53–
54, 55–56
Cinna (*Julius Caesar*), 112
City of God, The (Augustine), 22,
23
Civilization of the Renaissance in
Italy (Burckhardt), 63
Clement VII, Pope, 80, 81, 82
Cleombrotus, 22, 23
Cleopatra, 100
Commento sopra la Commedia
(Landino), 61
Coniurationis Commentarium
(Poliziano), 65, 67–70
Convivio (Dante), 27
Counter-Reformation, 92, 93

Dante (*see also Divine Comedy,
The*), 127n.31; Bruni on, 56, 57,
58–61; and Christian
philosophers compared, 22–26;
and Cicero compared, 21; and
clash between classical and
Christian values, 116;
condemnation of Brutus by, 2–
5, 15, 26, 29–30, 32, 35, 51, 53;
evaluation of ancient world by,
31–32; Giannotti on, 90–92; on
human freedom, 49; and
Humanists compared, 50, 51–
53; identification with Cato,
33–34; influence of, 1, 36, 38;
influence of Lucan on, 12–13;
Landino's commentary on, 61–
62; Machiavelli on, 70; as
medieval author, 35, 36–37;
and Petrarch compared, 40–41,

42; Stoics influence on, 14, 15,
16, 18; treatment of Caesar by,
2, 4, 26, 30–31, 35; on Ulysses
and Horace, 5–7; views on
suicide, 21–22, 26–30
De beneficiis (Seneca), 17–19
Decameron, The (Boccaccio), 45–48
De casibus birorum illustrium
(Boccaccio), 45–48
De constantia sapients (Seneca),
14–15
De fato et fortuna (Salutati), 50,
51–52, 55, 56
De Finibus (Cicero), 19, 21
De Gestis Caesaris (Petrarch), 41
De Libertate (Rinuccini), 65, 73–
75, 77–78
Della Robbia, Luca, 65, 76–79
De Monarchia (Dante), 3, 30–31,
35
De Officiis (Cicero), 20–21, 41
De Oratore (Cicero), 57
De rerum natura (Lucretius), 16
D'Este, Duke Alfonso II, 104–5
D'Este, Niccolo', 64
De Tyranno (Salutati), 24, 50, 51,
53–56, 57
Dialogi di Donato Giannotti de'
giorni che Dante consumo' nel
cercare l'Inferno e 'l Purgatorio
(Giannotti), 90–92, 93
Discorsi sopra la prima deca di Tito
Livio (Machiavelli), 70–73, 97,
99
Discorso o Dialogo intorno alla
nostra lingua (Machiavelli), 70
Divine Comedy, The (Dante) (*see
also* Dante), 7, 30, 35, 40, 52,
125n.1; Brutus' punishment in,
2–3, 51, 53; Cacciaguida in,
33–34; Caesar in, 31; Cato in,
8; Dante as character of, 33;
genre of, 25–26; Giannotti on,
90–92; influence of Lucan on,

13; Landino's commentary on, 61–62; suicide in, 7, 8, 22, 23, 26–30; Ulysses in, 5–6
Don Quixote (Cervantes), 36

Enlightenment, 60
Epicureanism, 16
Epistole (Horace), 6
Ercole, Duke, 64
Euleutherius. *See* Rinuccini, Alamanno
Euripides, 42

Ford, Franklin L., 77
Fourth Eclogue (Virgil), 3–4, 35

Gentile, Gerolamo, 64
Giannotti, Donato, 39, 65, 89–92, 93, 95
Ginori, Caterina Soderini, 88
Giucciardini, Francesco, 74
Gollancz, Israel, 119–20
Grévin, Jacques, 103–4, 105, 107, 110
Guicciardini, Francesco, 84, 99

Hamlet, 70, 80, 97–98, 119–24
Hamlet (Shakespeare), 1, 40, 104, 110, 119–24
Hamlet in Iceland (Gollancz), 119
Hamlet's Mill (de Santilliana), 120
Hercules, 14, 102
Hercules Oetaeus (Seneca), 102
Herder, Johann Gottfried von, 115
Historia Danica (Saxo), 119
History: vs. allegory, 26–32, 60; vs. literature, 24, 61; vs. myth, 60, 62, 65
Homer, 5
Horace, 6–7
Humanism (*see also* Renaissance), 1, 2; political attitudes of, 36–37, 44, 47, 49, 50

Il Convivio (Dante), 8
Inferno (Dante) (*see also Divine Comedy, The*), 2–3, 5, 28, 53, 125n.1
Innocent VII, Pope, 56

Jocasta, 46
John of Salisbury, 24–25, 26
Judas (*The Divine Comedy*), 2–3, 53
Julius Caesar (Muret), 101–3, 105, 107, 110
Julius Caesar (Shakespeare), 1, 40, 98, 111–15, 120; and *Hamlet* compared, 122–23; and Pescetti's *Cesare* compared, 104, 106, 110, 111

Laius, 46
La Mort de César (Voltaire), 115
Lampugnani, 64
Landino, Cristoforo, 61–62, 91
Leopardi, Giacomo, 115
Leo X, Pope, 76, 80
Life of Cato (Plutarch), 22–23
Lives (Plutarch), 111
Livy, 119, 120
Lollius, Maximus, 6
Lorenzaccio (de Musset), 81
Lucan, 1, 7–13, 27, 34, 98, 102; influence on Dante, 7–8, 12–13
Lucifer (*The Divine Comedy*), 2–3, 59, 90, 91
Lucretius, 16

Machiavelli, Niccolo', 39, 44, 65–66, 74, 89; on destiny, 50; influence of, 101, 122; and Pescetti compared, 105; on plots, 70–73, 80, 83, 96–97, 99; separation of politics from ethics by, 37, 47, 123; and Shakespeare compared, 111–12
Margaret of Absburg, 85

de' Medici, Alessandro, 38, 65, 80, 84–86, 99
de' Medici, Catherine, 80
de' Medici, Cosimo, 84, 89
de' Medici, Giovanni, 65
de' Medici, Giuliano, 64–65, 76, 78
de' Medici, Giulio, 65
de' Medici, Lorenzino, 65, 79–89, 97, 98, 101; contemporary accounts regarding, 38–39, 65, 81–85, 99; self-justification of, 65, 80, 85–87
de' Medici, Lorenzo, 64–65, 70, 73, 75, 76, 80
de' Medici, Pierfrancesco, 80
Michelangelo, ix, 38–39, 65, 81, 89–92, 93
Mini, Pier di ser, 58
Moro, Aldo, ix–x
Muret, Marc Antoine, 101–3, 105, 107, 110
de Musset, Alfred, 81
Myth, 60, 62, 65

Napoleon, 108
Nero, 27, 45, 85
Niccoli, Niccolo', 56–57, 58–61, 127n.31

Octavian, 99, 113
Odyssey (Homer), 5
Oedipus, ix–x, 46, 121
Oedipus the King (Sophocles), ix–x, 96, 123
Olgiati, Girolamo, 64, 67
Ophelia (*Hamlet*), 123

Paradise (Dante) (*see also Divine Comedy, The*), 33–34
Parricide, 46, 51; and Caesar's suspected paternity of Brutus, 44, 55, 67, 96, 109; and king as "father of state," 18–19, 44, 67, 96–97; as theme in tragedy, 50

Pascal, Blaise, 100
Pazzi, Francesco, 69
Pazzi, Jacopo, 68, 69
Pazzi conspiracy, 64–65, 67–70, 71, 73–75, 82, 113
Pescetti, Orlando, 104–10; and Shakespeare compared, 104, 106, 110, 111
Petrarch, 40–45; in Bruni's *Dialogus*, 56, 57, 58; and Salutati, 50, 53, 54
Phaedo (Plato), 22–23
Pharsalia (Lucan), 7–13, 98, 102; influence on Dante, 7–8, 12–13
Philippics (Cicero), 41
Pier della Vigna, 28
Pindarus (*Julius Caesar*), 113
Piso, 27
Plato, 16, 22–23, 24
Plutarch, 1, 30, 37, 58, 96, 130n.39; on Brutus' ambition, 67, 98, 100; on Brutus' intellectualism, 66–67, 74; on Cato, 13, 22–23, 34; as source for Shakespeare, 111, 113, 120
Political Murder: From Tyrannicide to Terrorism (Ford), 77
Politics (Aristotle), 97
Poliziano, Angelo, 65, 67–70, 71, 82, 113–14
Polonius (*Hamlet*), 121, 122
Polycraticus (John of Salisbury), 24–25
Pompey, 8, 9–10, 11, 96, 106
Prince, The (Machiavelli), 39, 50, 65, 66, 70, 80; on destiny, 50; influence of, 122; and Petrarch compared, 44; and Shakespeare's *Julius Caesar* compared, 111–12
Prose of Edda (Sturluson), 119
Puccinotti, Francesco, 88
Purgatory (Dante) (*see also Divine Comedy, The*), 35, 52, 90; Cato in, 7, 8, 22, 28–29

Quevado, Francisco de, 93

Renaissance (*see also* Humanism), 1, 2; decline of, 92–95; discussion on textuality during, 61; fascination with Roman history during, 48, 105; fashion during, 62–67; ideas about destiny during, 49–50, 51; monarchical power during, 111–12, 114–15; and morality of action, 21, 40–41; revival of classical culture during, 26; theatre during, 40, 110; transformation of Brutus story during, 31, 36–40; tyrannicide during, 38–39, 64–65, 67, 75–79

Ridolfi, Cardinal, 89

Rinuccini, Alamanno, 65, 73–75, 77–78

Rossi, Roberto, 56

Sallust, 67–68, 69, 71, 82, 113–14, 130n.39

Salutati, Coluccio, 24, 50–56; *De fato et fortuna*, 50, 51–52, 55, 56; *De Tyranno*, 24, 50, 51, 53–56, 57, 60

Salviati, Francesco, 64, 68–69

Salviati, Jacopo, 69

San Gallo, Bastiano da, 85

Sansoni, Raffaele Riario, 69

Santilliana, Giorgio de, 120

Savonarola, Girolamo, 76

Saxo Grammaticus, 119–20, 122

Seneca, 1, 16, 31, 102, 126n.24; on Brutus, 17–19; on Cato, 14–15; and Salutati compared, 51; suicide of, 27; on Ulysses, 6, 14–15

Servilia, 55, 96, 109

Sforza, Galeazzo Maria, 64, 67

Shakespeare, William (*see also Hamlet; Julius Caesar*), 1, 40, 98; and Pescetti compared, 104, 106, 110, 111; sources for, 104, 111, 119–20; view of power in plays of, 111–15, 122–23

Sixtus IV, Pope, 64

Socrates, 13, 23, 27, 29, 126n.24

Soderini, Maria, 80

Sophocles, x, 96

Source of Hamlet, The (Gollancz), 119

Spengler, Oswald, 108

Stoicism, 37; attitude toward death in, 14, 16, 34; Cicero's attitude toward, 19–20, 21; Dante's adherence to, 22, 26; individual freedom in, 14–16; in Pescetti's *Cesare*, 109, 110; on political evolution, 16–19, 109, 110; in Shakespeare's *Julius Caesar*, 114; virtue and destiny in, 6, 7, 8–12, 19–21

Storia Fiorentina (Varchi), 81

Strozzi, Filippo, 82

Sturluson, Snorri, 119

Suetonius, 1, 55, 67, 96

Suicide, 17; Christian view of, 22–24, 27, 30, 34; Dante's view of, 7–8, 21–22, 26–30, 32, 33, 34

Tacitus, 92–93, 96, 101

Tarquin the Proud, 57, 58, 100, 106–7, 119, 120

Tragedy, 1; clash between action and thought in, 40; collective guilt in, 10; futility of action in, 100; Grévin's *César* as, 104; *Hamlet* as, 123; medieval view of, 4; Muret's *Julius Caesar* as, 102–3; vs. omniscient mode, 12–13; parricide theme in, 44, 50; Pescetti's *Cesare* as, 110

Tusculan Disputations (Cicero), 22

Tyrannicide (*see also* Pazzi conspiracy): in Boccaccio, 46;

Cicero's view of, 20–21; Florentine republicans on, 90–92; John of Salisbury's view of, 24–25; in modern society, 123–24; during Renaissance, 38–39, 64–65, 67, 75–79; Stoic view of, 19

Ulysses, 5–6, 7, 14, 30

Varchi, Benedetto, 81, 82–83
Vasari, Giorgio, 85
Virgil, 1, 3–4, 28–29, 59, 125n.1
Visconti, 64
Vita (Cellini), 84–85
Voltaire, 115

War with Catiline (Sallust), 67–68

Zeno, 126n.24

Manfredi Piccolomini is Associate Professor of Italian at Lehman College of the City University of New York. He also teaches Italian cultural history at Barnard College/Columbia University. A graduate of the University of Florence and of Harvard, Professor Piccolomini previously taught at Vassar. He has written two other books on art and on literature: *Il mondo delle aste, collezionismo e mercato dell'arte* and *Il pensiero estetico di Gianvincenzo Gravina.*